To. Kim.

love Mal

Aug 99.

D0832949

The Observers Series
CATS

About the Book

Though the history of the domestic cat goes back at least to the time of the ancient Egyptians, it is only comparatively recently that scientific breeding has been undertaken to produce the many beautiful varieties seen on the show bench today.

All the recognized breeds and varieties are described and illustrated in this book, as well as many new varieties about to receive recognition. Owners of the 'household pet' as well as of pedigree animals will find useful advice on care and breeding, and from her experience as a judge at many cat shows the author gives valuable hints on entering and preparing a cat for show. A list is also given of the main cat clubs and societies in Britain.

About the Author

Grace Pond gained recognition as an international cat judge, and as the organizer of the National Cat Club Show. She was President of the Governing Council of the Cat Fancy and a delegate. She organized shows for other clubs, and became a Patron of several overseas clubs and a President or Vice-President of several clubs in Britain. For more than thirty years she bred Blue Persians and some British shorthairs, often appearing on television and radio programmes relating to cats. She is the author of nearly thirty books on cat care and breeding, several of which have been translated into other languages.

OBSERVERS

CATS

Grace Pond

Photographs by **Marc Henrie**

PENGUIN BOOKS

Published by the Penguin Group
Penguin Books Ltd, 27 Wrights Lane, London W8 5TZ, England
Penguin Books USA Inc., 375 Hudson Street, New York, New York 10014, USA
Penguin Books Australia Ltd, Ringwood, Victoria, Australia
Penguin Books Canada Ltd, 10 Alcorn Avenue, Toronto, Ontario, Canada
M4V 3B2
Penguin Books (NZ) Ltd, 182–190 Wairau Road, Auckland 10, New Zealand

Penguin Books Ltd, Registered Offices: Harmondsworth, Middlesex, England

This edition first published in Great Britain in 1959 by
Frederick Warne

This revised edition published in 1996 by Claremont Books,
an imprint of Godfrey Cave Associates Limited,
42 Bloomsbury Street, London WC1B 3QJ

ISBN 1 85471 028 1

Printed in Italy

CONTENTS

A prize-winning Colourpoint

INTRODUCTION

The first edition of this book appeared over thirty years ago, and looking back now I am amazed how the Cat Fancy has grown beyond all expectation throughout the world. There are many new varieties of pedigree cats, and where once cat breeders numbered a hundred or so, there are now thousands. The number of cat shows in Britain has trebled and it is almost the same in other countries. Many of the shows are judged by international cat judges (some of them from Britain) who are now world famous. The number of entries at the shows increases all the time and where once show managers were worried about getting enough cats to fill the hall, the chief worry nowadays is getting a large enough hall to take all the cats and kittens, and most shows have to return entries because of lack of space.

Pedigree cats have become more and more popular, as I know from the correspondence I receive from all over the world asking about the varieties, where to get them and how to care for them. Would-be owners are sometimes worried about taking on a pedigree kitten, thinking that such an exotic creature needs special care and attention; but given affection, attention and good feeding, pedigree cats live just as normal a life as any mongrel cat. Barring accidents they live just as long – several of my longhairs reaching seventeen years – and I have known of some that lived to nineteen and even twenty-one years.

The object of this book is to enable the reader to recognize any particular variety of pedigree cat at a glance and to help any would-be owner in the choice of variety. There are also chapters on care, showing and breeding.

One should also remember that the same care and attention should be given to the far-from-humble mongrel, the pet of the house, found in all colours and coat patterns. All cats, after all, have the same common ancestors, and it is by the selective breeding of cats of unknown parentage not much more than a century ago that we have all the exotic creatures which appear at today's cat shows.

ACKNOWLEDGEMENTS

The author wishes to thank Mrs. A. Ashford, Mrs. D. Clarke, Mrs. D. Hoyle, Mrs. E. Menezes, Mrs. B. Nicholas, Miss P. Turner, Mrs. M. Turney and Miss M. Swift for information on some of the varieties.

The author is also grateful to Marc Henrie for taking and supplying the colour photographs illustrating the varieties, and to the owners for allowing their cats and kittens to be photographed.

Thanks are also due to the Governing Council of the Cat Fancy for permission to reproduce the standards.

Norwegian Forest cats

THE CAT FAMILY

'Cat' is the general name given to all members of the feline or Felidae family. It may seem strange to some that the homely creature sitting so peacefully by the fire belongs to the same family as the lion, tiger, puma, leopard, lynx and ocelot, as well as the smaller, more closely allied species. They are carnivores or flesh eaters, animals which stalk and devour living prey; they vary greatly in size from the lion, which may measure as much as ten feet from head to tail, to the little spotted cat of India, sometimes smaller than the average domestic cat.

Felines have many common characteristics: the shortness of their muzzles, the supple movements of the forepaws and the strong curved and retractable claws. They have long lithe bodies combining strength and agility. They are digitigrade, that is, they walk on their toes. This makes them light of foot, stealthy and silent of approach in stalking prey. The skulls of the various species of true cat are similar and uniform in shape. Their tongues are covered with small, rasp-like surfaces called papillae, and are used for licking flesh from bones and cleaning the coat. In adult animals the teeth number thirty, and are adapted for holding prey and cutting up flesh with a scissor-like action. They are not suitable for breaking and cracking bones. The whiskers are long bristle-like hairs, connected to nerves and they act as very sensitive organs of perception. The hearing is acute. The eyes are large and full, with pupils that can expand or contract to slits according to the density of the light. Cats cannot see in total darkness, but their eyes are responsive to the smallest gleams of light. Their tails are usually long and round, and can be used most expressively in portraying the emotions, particularly when the cat is excited or chasing prey.

The actual origin of the domestic cat is hidden in the mists of antiquity and much is still a matter of conjecture rather than fact. For many years it was assumed that the domestic cat was the wild cat tamed, but it is now agreed that they are two distinct breeds, although there are cases of a domestic cat running wild and interbreeding with the wild species.

Similar to many of the domestic tabbies in general colouring, the wild cat, once known in many parts of the British Isles and Europe, is now a comparative rarity except in the Highlands of Scotland. There it is not so widespread as once, due to its habit of preying on livestock and game, and its subsequent destruction. The wild cat is easily distinguishable by its superior size and strength, being up to three feet in length. The head too is large and square with abundant whiskers, and the coat is yellowish-grey with a dark streak running along the back and down the short bushy tail, which does not taper, but is nearly uniform in thickness from the top to the tip.

Many attempts have been made to tame a specimen but either the kittens have succumbed to illness when brought into contact with other animals, or if they have lived, they have failed to respond to kindness. It has been found that even if the kittens are brought up by hand they are still quite vicious, needing to be handled in gloves. At the first official cat show a wild cat was a big attraction, but it had to stay in its travelling box as, in spite of the efforts and endeavours of ten men, it could not be got out of the box and into the exhibition cage prepared for it.

The Indian desert cat is of particular interest to scientists in that it is known to interbreed with the local domestic cats, many of which carry similar markings. It is thought possible that the domestic cats in India originated from this species.

HISTORY OF THE DOMESTIC CAT

Experts still differ about the origin of the domestic cat, but many think that its true ancestor was the caffre cat of Egypt, which the Egyptians tamed and trained and used for hunting. The first definite evidence of the existence of the domestic cat comes from ancient Egypt, from over three thousand years ago, although it may have been known in the world long before this.

Held in great esteem, it was worshipped in the temples, protected from injury, loved during life, and at death was mourned by the entire family, who frequently shaved off their eyebrows as a sign of mourning. Both rich and poor had the bodies of their cats embalmed, sometimes in finest linen, and placed in mummy cases, often richly decorated and lined with gold leaf. Many museums have examples of these mummified cats and cases.

The Egyptians realized the cat's immense value in protecting the granaries from the ravages of rats and mice. Cat motifs were used constantly in ornamentation and decoration, and small models of cats appeared on amulets and scarabs; many figures of cats, made of bronze, copper, faience, gold and rare and valuable wood have been found, some wearing gold earrings and elaborate necklaces.

From the models and statuettes found these early cats seem to have been even longer and slimmer than the Siamese of today. Many are depicted with markings something like those of tabbies. Even in those days there appear to have been two distinct types – the big eared and long-nosed and the short-eared and blunt-nosed, very much as seen today.

In India cats were mentioned in the Sanskrit writings over two thousand years ago, while in China in about 500 BC Confucius is known to have had a favourite cat. About AD 600 Mohammed is said to have preached with a cat in his arms, while at about the same time in Japan cats were kept in the temples to guard the sacred manuscripts, presumably from the ravages of rats and mice.

It is surmised that the Romans brought the first domestic cats to Britain and bones have been found in the ruins of Roman villas. The wild cat was hunted, but the rare domestic cat was much prized. With the advent of the middle ages, in England and in many other parts of the world the once revered cat became an animal to look on with fear and dread. It became the victim of sacrifice and ceremonies connected with black magic. Witches were pictured with cats riding on their broomsticks and were even said to be able to turn themselves into cats. Black cats in particular were picked out as being the familiars of the Devil and many were wilfully destroyed. In France cats were publicly burned as sacrifices until the practice was forbidden by law during the reign of Louis XIII.

Gradually the witch-hunts died down and the cat was again looked on with favour and was allowed to sit by the fire and to go about its true pursuit of killing rats and mice. Many famous people, including Dr Johnson and Victor Hugo, were devoted to their cats, although Napoleon is said to have detested them. In the Victorian period the cat came very much into its own. There were cat pictures, cat books, cards and calendars. Lewis Carroll portrayed the disappearing Cheshire cat in *Alice in Wonderland* and Louis Wain, afterwards to become a cat judge, became well known for his cartoons and cat sketches in children's books. The cats' meat man became a well-known character with his stall in the market place selling half-pennyworths of meat on skewers for cats.

In 1871 the first official cat show was organized at Crystal Palace by Harrison Weir. This became an annual event, and roused people's interest in cats and cat breeding. Breeders endeavoured to produce different varieties and the first pedigrees were written. The two wars, with the consequent food shortages, had severe effects on breeding, but the cat recovered as ever, and today is even more popular.

Cats are now almost an industry on their own, and if an ancient Egyptian were to return today, he might well feel that we too worship the cat. There are factories turning out millions of tons of tinned food and medicines for cats, and all kinds of cat accessories. Cats appear constantly on television in plays and advertisements. There are innumerable books about them, both fiction and non-fiction. There are also thousands of pottery and china cats. Indeed, with the number of cat shows for both pedigree and pet cats increasing all the time, silver cups and trophies being awarded for the best, and with prizewinning stock being eagerly sought after throughout the world, cats are definitely in.

TABLE OF CAT VARIETIES

Numerical Index of Breeds

Longhaired cats

Shorthaired cats

Top left – *Longhair: Red Tabby;* top right – *Shorthair: Red Tabby;* bottom left – *Siamese: Blue-point;* bottom right – *Balinese: Tortie-point*

LONGHAIRED CATS

Shorthaired cats have been known in Europe from Roman times, but it was not until the end of the sixteenth century that cats with long fur made their appearance. It is claimed that Nicholas Claude Fabri de Peirese, a naturalist, scientist and archaeologist, introduced the Angora cats to France about this time. The longhairs of today were evolved from the Angoras and from other longcoated cats from Persia, and there are now many varieties with different coloured fur and coat patterns.

The standard for the majority of longhairs is much the same. (For every recognized cat variety there is a standard, against which one hundred points are allocated for the characteristics required for what would be considered the perfect cat.) The colourings may differ, but the coats should be long and flowing without woolliness. A distinctive feature is the full ruff or frill. This is the long hair around the head, which is brushed up until if forms a frame for the round broad head. The ears must be small, round-tipped, set well apart. The eyes may be of different colours according to the variety but they must be large, round, wideawake eyes, and not deep set. The nose must be short and broad, almost snub, with a distinct stop. The body should be low and cobby, with short thick legs, and the tail or brush short and very full.

These cats are in no way delicate and need no special upbringing. Their long coats call for constant attention, but their owners are adequately repaid for their labours, for a well-groomed longhaired cat in perfect condition always attracts admiration and is essential when shown.

PERSIAN SELF BLACK LONGHAIR   1

One of the oldest varieties in Britain, the Black is still comparatively rare. The first Blacks shown, in about 1890, were Imp and Satan, exhibited by the Hon. Mrs McLaran Morrison; Satan was never beaten at any show. The early Blacks frequently had big ears and long noses, being more Angora in type. Selective breeding with other varieties, in

Black longhair

particular the Blues, much improved the type, producing the outstanding specimens seen at some of the shows today, several of which have been Best in Show. Before and between the two wars this was a variety that attracted much attention at the shows, but for some reason the numbers have not increased greatly since then.

The kittens are born black, but frequently within a few weeks the coats turn rusty, and white or grey hairs appear in the fur. With age these hairs and the rustiness disappear and the lovely dense black colouring is seen, improving as the cat reaches maturity and grows the adult coat. As all kittens are born with blue eyes, it may be a few months before they change completely to the deep orange or copper colouring required.

Black to Black breeding is often used, but outcrosses are still used to improve the type, Blues and Whites giving the most success. Blacks may sire outstanding Whites and may be used as studs for Tortoiseshells, Tortoiseshell-and-whites, Smokes, Creams and Bi-colours.

The Black is probably one of the most difficult cats to keep looking immaculate, and daily grooming is a must. Unfortunately the black fur reacts quickly to damp and may soon

17

take on a brownish hue. It also reacts to strong sunlight, the coat tending to take on a bleached look. Talcum powder should never be used in grooming; some fanciers sprinkle a few drops of bay rum well down into the roots of the fur, brushing it well out and polishing the coat afterwards with a chamois leather or silk handkerchief.

There are many superstitions associated with Black cats, both longhaired and shorthaired. In Britain they are considered lucky, but in other countries it is entirely the reverse. In the middle ages they were looked on as witches' cats and familiars of the Devil, and credited with supernatural powers. This may explain the association with bad luck. Certainly, although they are usually good tempered and make excellent pets, a Black preparing for a fight with its large orange eyes blazing and practically every hair standing on end can be an awesome sight.

The type should be as for all longhairs, with a good broad head, large round eyes, small ears, cobby body and full short tail, and is frequently very good.

STANDARD (with scale of points)

Coat	Including colour, texture and quality; eveness of colour. Lustrous dense black, sound and even in colour, free from rustiness, shading, white hairs or markings. Nose leather, eye rims and paw pads black	40 points
Body	Including shape, size and bone structure, length of tail, height, thickness of legs and paws.	20 points
Head	Including general shape of head, forehead; set of eyes, nose length, width and stop; width of cheeks and muzzle; chin.	25 points
Eyes	Including size, shape and colour which should be copper or deep orange.	15 points
Note	Awards are withheld for any solid areas of white anywhere on any Persian Self Longhair (except in white cats). In Kitten Open Classes certificates are withheld for the following: incorrect or extremely pale eye colour;	

incorrect pigment in nose leather, eye rims or paw pads;
almond or oriental eye shape and/or set.

White longhair : blue-eyed

PERSIAN SELF WHITE LONGHAIR 2,2a,2b

According to old books on cats, the first with long fur seen in Europe, as long ago as the sixteenth century, were the Whites; they came from Turkey and were known as Angoras after the city now called Ankara. They arrived in Britain via France, and so were also known as French cats.

Many of these early Whites were blue-eyed, and some appeared to be dull, unresponsive, sullen cats, until it was realized that they were deaf. Their heads were narrow, the ears large and upright, the noses long and straight and the fur long and silky.

Following the Angoras came the Persians. They too had

White longhair: oranged-eyed

long fur but the coats tended to be woollier, and the colours various. They were heavier in build, with broader heads and smaller ears. Crossbreeding between the Angoras and the Persians resulted in the almost complete disappearance of the Angora type, so much so that at the beginning of the twentieth century a breeder wrote that she had no definite information as to the difference between the Persians and Angoras.

It is interesting to note that in the United States the original Angoras, now known as the Turkish Angoras, have been reintroduced from Turkey, and that they are now accepted in Britain (breed 62). These Angoras are finer-boned cats with long silky coats: the heads are small to medium in size, tapering towards the chin; the ears are long and pointed, and the tails longish.

Deafness does still occur in the Whites, more particularly in the blue-eyed. Presumably there is a connection with albinism as deafness occurs in other all-white animals. The odd-eyed variety, that is with one blue and one orange eye, may be deaf on the blue-eyed side, but have hearing on the orange-eyed side. It should be stressed that not all blue-eyed Whites are deaf, although it may be very difficult to test for

White longhair : odd eyed

STANDARD

The basic standard and the scale of points is as described on page 18 for the Black Longhair.

Colour
: Pure white, free from marks of shade of any kind. Nose leather, eye rims and paw pads pink.

Eyes
: Blue-eyed white: decidedly blue, deeper shades preferred. Orange-eyed white: copper or deep orange. Odd-eyed white: one eye blue and one eye orange or deep copper.

Ears
: Small, round tipped, set wide on the head, fitting into the rounded contour of the head, with full ear furnishings but not unduly open at the base.

Note
: White kittens sometimes have some coloured hairs on the head and should not be penalized for this.

White longhair kitten: orange-eyed

The feet and paws may become soiled, but if this happens a little warm soapy water, a rinse and a quick dry will soon put matters right. As with all varieties, whether longhaired or shorthaired, the tail of the White must be kept free from grease, which tends to make it yellow. Males seem to be the most affected, and daily grooming may be necessary to keep the tail as pure white as the rest of the coat. Many breeders bath their White exhibits a few days before the show. The coat is not so affected by the sun as those of several of the other longhairs, nor does the fur turn shady, as does that of the Blues.

The kittens may have a pinkish appearance when newly born, but this is lost as the fur grows, and in a very short time they are rushing around looking like animated powder puffs.

The standard for the three varieties is the same, except for the eye colouring. Because of the wider selection given by their sheer numbers, the Orange-eyed Whites do seem to have better type, although it is only fair to say that there are really striking examples of all three varieties to be seen at the shows.

STANDARD

Colour	Pure white, without mark or shade of any kind.
Coat	Long and flowing on the body, full frill and brush, which should be short and broad; the coat should be close and soft and silky, not woolly in texture.
Body	Cobby and massive, without being coarse, with plenty of bone and substance, and low on the leg.
Head	Round and broad, with plenty of space between the ears, which should be small, neat and well covered; short nose, full cheeks and broad muzzle. An undershot jaw shall be considered a defect.
Eyes	Large, round and wide open, deep blue, or orange or copper in colour. If odd-eyed, one deep blue and one orange or copper.
Note	White kittens sometimes have some coloured hairs on the head and should not be penalized for this.

White longhair: odd-eyed

PERSIAN SELF BLUE LONGHAIR 3

The Blue longhair or Blue Persian, as it is still frequently referred to in most countries, was one of the earliest varieties to be recognized, and is still probably the most popular of the longhairs. With a broad head, tiny ears, short broad nose, round deep orange or copper coloured eyes, cobby body on short legs, well tufted feet, and a short full tail, the Blue is a beautiful creature – particularly when one sees an outstanding specimen coming very close to the approved standard.

At the first shows, unlike the Black and White, they did not have a class of their own, but appeared as 'Any Other Variety', as most had some white or tabby markings. Later they were shown in a class for Blue Tabbies and Blues with or without white, but in 1889 they had made such headway, due to careful breeding, that the class became 'Blue – Self-Coloured'. This lead to a considerable increase in entries and by 1890 separate classes were put on for the males and the females, although the kittens were still shown in the same class as the Blacks and Whites.

In 1894 a male, Wooloomooloo, owned by Mrs W. Hawkins, was said to be 'a grand blue', and as a stud was responsible for many outstanding kittens. His name appears on the pedigrees of many prizewinning blues today.

In 1901 Miss Frances Simpson, a well-known breeder and judge, founded the Blue Persian Club which drew up a standard for the Blues which was far-seeing and has required very little change ever since. Many of these early Blues had green eyes, but careful breeding with only those having the best eye colouring produced cats with the deep orange or copper eyes required. However, green rims are sometimes seen in present day cats, and this counts as a fault. A kink in the tail is a bad fault, and many fanciers consider that any Blue having a kinked tail should not be used for breeding, as this feature could continue to appear in future generations.

When first born the kittens, as in other pale self-coloured varieties may have tabby markings. These will gradually disappear as the kittens grow older.

The type of the Blue Persian has improved greatly over the years, so much so that it is frequently used in crossbreeding to improve other much admired varieties. They are used to produce the much admired Blue-creams. Mated to a Cream female, a Blue male will sire Blue-creams (which are female) and Cream males, while a Blue female mated to a Cream male may have Blue-creams and Blue males. A Blue male mated to a Blue-cream female may produce Blue females. Blue-creams, Blue males and Cream males.

STANDARD

The basic standard and the scale of points is as described on page 18 for the Black Longhair.

Colour   Medium to pale, blue, sound and even in colour, free from shading, markings or white hairs. A dark or slate grey coat should be considered very undesirable. Nose leather, eye rims and paw pads blue-grey.

Eyes   Copper or deep orange.

Paws   Large round firm paws, preferably well tufted. Toes carried close; five in front, four behind.

PERSIAN RED SELF LONGHAIR   4

A true Red Self is among the most beautiful of all the longhair
varieties, but it is also one of the most difficult to breed really
close to the recognized standards, as invariably there are
tabby markings somewhere on the head or body. In the early
days of cat breeding, the Reds were referred to as the Oranges,
and it is presumed that the colouring was not the deep rich
red now seen in some of the outstanding cats at the shows. At
the early shows, the judges' reports said that these Oranges
were self-coloured with a few tabby markings, but as the
classes were for 'Orange, marked and unmarked', it really did
not matter. By 1910 the colour had obviously improved, and
the classes were for 'Red or Orange, with separate classes for
the tabbies, by 1915, the word 'Orange' had disappeared, the
classes being for 'Red or Shaded' and for 'Red Tabbies'.

Of recent years there has been a revival of interest in the
variety with the result that by careful breeding there has
been a great improvement in both type and colour.
Nevertheless there are a very few without some form of
marking particularly on the face.

It is a fallacy to say that all Reds, whether longhair or
shorthair, are males for this is the case only when the mother

26

is not pure Red bred. When the breeding is from pure Red on both sides, any litters born may contain male and female kittens. Reds may be used in the breeding of Tortoiseshells and Tortoiseshell–and-whites, and also Cameos. A black male mated to a Tortoiseshell may produce Red-and-tortoiseshells.

Reds and Red Tabbies may be born in the same litter, and it is difficult to know at first which they are, as they will probably all have some tabby markings. They may or may not go as the kittens grow, and it may be some months before the breeder can be quite certain which is which.

The type nowadays is usually very good, the heads being broad and round, the ears small, the noses short and the big round eyes a deep copper colour. Faults are tabby markings on the face and rings on the tail.

STANDARD

The basic standard and the scale of points is as described on page 18 for the Black Longhair.

Colour	Deep rich red, free from white hairs, sound and even in colour, although slight shading on the forehead and legs is acceptable. Nose leather, eye rims and paw pads deep pink.
Eyes	Copper or deep orange.

Young Red longhair

PERSIAN SELF CREAM LONGHAIR 5

This variety was once regarded as a sport, as it arose in the first place from accidental matings between Blue and Red (then known as Orange), or else from Tortoiseshell. Such cats were referred to as Fawns, as they probably were in those days; they were considered of little value and were neutered and sold as pets, being called Spoiled Oranges. Little was understood then about selective breeding for particular colours, but a few were sent to America, were the importance of using them in breeding was appreciated much earlier.

The first Fawn recorded was Cupid Bassanio in 1890, but there is no record of any kittens by him. Later British fanciers became interested in the colour, but as they bred from Tortoiseshells and Red Tabbies it was mostly males that resulted, while the few females for some reason proved to be bad breeders; the type too was bad, the ears being tall and the noses long. Eventually, by more or less hit-and-miss matings, it came to be realized that matings to Blues produced the best results and that Cream males and females could be produced to order. It is now known that a Cream female mated to a Blue male can have Cream males and Blue-cream females; a Cream male mated to a Blue-cream female may have both male and female Cream kittens. Blue male kittens

Cream longhair kittens

and Blue-cream kittens in the same litter.

Right from the beginning America was much more enthusiastic about the Creams, and a number crossed the Atlantic, one of whom was the famous Kew Laddie. He sired a number of outstanding kittens. Creams are still one of the most popular varieties in North America, many winning the highest awards. As regards type they tend to have even shorter noses than many seen in Britain. (This applies not only to the Creams but also to other longhaired varieties.)

Colour is very important, as it should be pure, sound and even all over, without shading. Unfortunately the 'hot' or reddish tinge, which is a fault, does appear frequently, especially when careful consideration is not given to the choice of matings and the effects of mixing certain lines together. It is of great importance to study the pedigrees and to endeavour to find the good and bad points of the available cats; the stud that is selected for the female should be the best possible, as bad faults are easily brought into a strain, but prove exceedingly difficult to breed out.

There is a tendency for bars and faint tabby markings to appear in kittens. These may fade, but if they persist in the adult cat it is a definite fault, as is a white tip to the tail, a pale undercoat instead of pure cream throughout, and any 'hotness' in the coat.

Creams are used in matings to Tortoiseshells, Tortoiseshell-and-whites, Blacks and Blues. An occasional Blue outcross is recommended as Cream to Cream indefinitely may mean loss of type.

STANDARD

The basic standard and the scale of points is as described on page 18 for the Black Longhair.

Colour   Pale to medium cream, sound and even in colour, without a white undercoat, free from shading, markings or white hair. Nose leather, eye rims and paw pads pink.

Eyes   Copper or deep orange.

BLACK SMOKE LONGHAIR 6

The Smoke is one of the most unusual varieties, but at first glance it may well be mistaken for a Black, as it is not until the cat moves that the striking contrast of the white undercoat shading to black at the tips may be seen. The body shades to silver on the sides; the frill and ear tufts should be silver and the mask black. There should be no sign of tabby markings.

Although the Smoke is one of the oldest varieties, thought to have originated by mixed breeding of Blacks, Whites and Blues, it is still one of the rarest of the longhairs, perhaps because of the difficulty of breeding really outstanding specimens. Smoke may be mated to Smoke, but this may eventually result in loss of type. Some have been produced by cross-breeding with Blacks.

Kittens are born black with little or no white and it takes a very experienced breeder to determine which are Smokes and which are Blacks. In fact they have frequently been registered as Blacks, only to grow into the most beautiful Smokes.

Smokes require constant grooming, to prevent their striking appearance being spoiled by shaggy coats. Like

Blue Smoke longhair

Blacks, the kittens may go through a rusty stage before the true coat is seen. Furthermore the coats react to strong sunlight and damp. To exhibit a Smoke looking at its very best takes many weeks of expert grooming and then waiting until the contrasts are really showing to advantage.

BLUE SMOKE LONGHAIR   6a

The Blue Smoke is another variety, which has the same distinctive white undercoat, but blue colouring in the place of black. It is a very pretty variety, with many admirers, but still comparatively few in numbers at the shows.

STANDARD (with scale of points)

A Smoke is a cat of contrasts, the undercoat being as ash-white as possible, with the tips shading to black, the dark points being most defined on the back, head and feet, and the light points on frill, flanks and ear tufts.

Body   Cobby body, not coarse but massive, short legs.

                                       15 points

Head	Broad and round width between the ears, which should be small and tufted; snub nose.
	20 points
Eyes	Orange or copper in colour, large and round in shape with a pleasing expression. 10 points
Tail	Short and bushy. 5 points
Coat	Of silky texture, long and dense with extra long frill. For texture and condition. 10 points
Colour	As described above the points awarded for body mask and feet, frill and ear tufts and undercoat.
	40 points

Other recognized smoke varieties are as follows:

Chocolate Smoke (breed number 6b) – chocolate shading to silver on the sides and flanks. Mask and feet chocolate with no markings. Frill and ear tufts silver. Undercoat as nearly white as possible.

Lilac Smoke (breed number 6c) – as for chocolate, above, except lilac.

Red Smoke (breed number 6d) – body red shading to white on the sides and flanks. Mask and feet red with no markings. Frill and ear tufts white. Undercoat as nearly white as possible. Tabby markings not permitted.

Tortie Smoke (breed number 6e) – tipping to comprise black, red and cream broken into patches.

Blue-cream Smoke (breed number 6g) – tipping to consist of blue and cream softly intermingled. Any intensity acceptable. Nose leather blue, pink or combination of the two.

Chocolate Tortie Smoke (breed number 6j) and Lilac Tortie Smoke (breed number 6j) are also now recognized.

Blue Tabby longhair

TABBY LONGHAIR

The first cats referred to as domestic are thought to have had tabby markings; and it is said that if all the domestic cats in the world were mated with one another eventually all cats would be tabbies of some kind or another. It is therefore surprising how difficult it can be to breed a pedigree tabby with the correct pattern of markings, particularly in the case of the longhairs.

There is very little proven history about the background of any of the cats with long fur, but Harrison Weir, the organizer of the first official cat show and himself a cat judge always said that the longhaired tabbies did not come from Angora (Ankara) or Persia, but had evolved from matings between the already resident shorthairs.

The name tabby is derived from Attabiya, a district in Baghdad were watered silk was made centuries ago. The silk, with its distinctive striped pattern, was called tabbisilk in England and as the cats bore a similar pattern they came to be known as tabby cats.

There were originally three recognized varieties of Longhair Tabbies, Silver, Brown and Red, but led by America a further seven are recognized. Tabby markings for both long and short fur are the same and as may be imagined, this classic coat pattern is more clearly defined in the short coats than the long and is, therefore, described in the section of Shorthair Tabbies on page 87.

Silver Tabby longhair

SILVER TABBY LONGHAIR 7

This was once such a popular variety that one could commonly find as many as 28 or more entries in a show; nowadays, in Britain at least, it is less common and there are usually only about six entries in a show. This is a great pity as a Silver Tabby with the dense black markings showing up against a true silver background colouring is a beautiful animal. It is sometimes said that as the number of Chinchillas increased the Silver Tabbies decreased. It is thought that the Chinchillas originated through the Silvers, but nothing definite can be proved, as unfortunately the early breeders do not appear to have kept any records of their breeding programmes, nor could anyone have possibly realized the interest there would be in the future in pedigree cat breeding.

Some very good examples are now appearing at the shows, with good dense black markings on the silver ground colour, but the numbers have not greatly increased as yet.

It was the opinion of one early breeder of the Silvers that the variety started to deteriorate when the green eye became the standard, and it was thought then that if the old hazel eye colour were to return, it would be a great incentive to breeders. Today's standard does say 'green or hazel', and there is definitely some improvement.

Any brown tinge in the coat is a fault, as is any yellow or brown around the lips or on the face. It is acknowledged that this is one of the most difficult of the longhaired cats to produce to perfection.

STANDARD (with scale of points)

Head	Round and broad with plenty of space between well-tufted ears, which should be small, neat and well covered. Short broad nose with a slope that is not extreme. Full cheeks, muzzle and no pitch.	25 points
Eyes	Wide open, large and round.	15 points
Body	Cobby, muscular with short thick sturdy legs and full well furnished tail.	20 points
Coat	Markings clearly defined with no brindling; letter 'M' on forehead. The points are awarded for colour, markings and condition.	40 points

Other Tabby Longhairs now recognized through not fully described here are Blue Tabby (breed number 8a), Chocolate Tabby (breed number 8b), Lilac Tabby (breed number 8c), Tortie Tabby (breed number 8e), Blue Tortie Tabby (breed number 8g), Chocolate Tortie Tabby (breed number 8h) and Lilac Tortie Tabby (breed number 8j).

BROWN TABBY LONGHAIR 8

Although tabbies of every colour may be found among house pets, and tabby markings have a tendency to crop up in the wrong pedigree breeds, to produce a longhaired Brown Tabby with the correct markings is far from easy. In the 1930s there were some very handsome examples with rich tawny sable coats and dense black markings, but the Second World War caused a virtual cessation of cat breeding in Britain from which some varieties never recovered. In consequence several are still comparatively scarce, and very few Brown Tabbies appear to have correct colouring.

There is a demand for Brown Tabbies as pets, but comparatively few appear at the shows. It should be remembered that it is difficult to get the exact markings required that it is difficult to get the exact markings required for a kitten to win on the show bench, whereas incorrect markings make no difference in an otherwise delightful pet. There have been one or two outstanding examples exhibited, but usually the black markings are not well defined and the type could be bettered.

At birth the kittens may appear to be heavily marked, while the ground colouring may be good. When teething is over, and as the fur grows, the stripes will possibly become more distinct and the background colour clearer. From a breeding point of view, it is wisest to keep the kitten with the cobbiest body, the best type head and the richest colouring. Faults are blurring of the markings, too solid markings on the back, a white chin and a white tip to the tail. The pattern of the markings is as for the other tabbies, while the background colour should be a rich tawny sable, and the markings a dense black.

STANDARD

The basic standard and scale of points is as described on page 36 for the Silver Tabby Longhair.

Colour	Rich tawny sable ground colour with dense black markings. Nose leather, brick red. Paw pads black or brown. White anywhere or a solid back are considered faults.
Coat	Long and flowing, tail short and full.
Body	Cobby and massive, short legs.
Head	Round and broad; small well-placed and well-tufted ears, short broad nose, full round cheeks.
Eyes	Large and round, orange or copper colour (no green rim).

Brown Tabby longhair

Red Tabby and Tortoiseshell longhair kittens

RED TABBY LONGHAIR 9

The Red Tabby is a fascinating cat with rich copper red colouring. This variety must never be confused with the Ginger Tabby pets, which are most attractive, but whose colour is quite sandy by comparison. As with all tabbies, the markings are most important and must be carried right down the back and the sides. A solid back is a bad fault and would count against a cat when exhibited. The markings must be dark red and the body colour a rich red.

The variety was once considered to be of very poor type, with narrow head and tall ears; however, careful breeding has ensured that there are now some beautiful examples on the show bench, with good broad heads and neat small well placed ears, and large round wide-open copper eyes. A small eye, which is often deepset as well, detracts from a good cat.

One of the worst faults, and also one of the hardest to breed out, is a white tip to the tail. White stars under the chin, on the chest or low down on the stomach are also faults which sometimes appear. Care should be taken when breeding to use a stud with deep-red colour and markings, and if possible with no white.

Red Tabbies make delightful colourful pets and are intelligent and very affectionate.

STANDARD

The basic standard and scale of points is as described on page 36 for the Silver Tabby Longhair.

Colour   Rich red ground colour with markings of deeper richer red. Nose leather and paw pads deep pink. White anywhere or a solid red back are considered faults.

Eyes   Large and round, orange or copper colour (no green rim). Certificates are withheld for any incorrect eye colour.

CHINCHILLA   10

The Chinchilla is one of the loveliest of the longhaired varieties, and in recent years has grown in popularity. This is most noticeable at the shows; at one event alone 42 adults and 76 kittens were entered.

At one time there was a great shortage of Chinchilla studs in Britain, but by a combination of breeding and importing from the USA the numbers have been built up, and plenty of kittens are being produced today.

The Chinchilla differs from other longhairs, such as the Blues, Creams and Whites, in that it is a daintier cat, smaller in physique but yet still compact and cobby, with the body set low on short sturdy legs. Chinchillas were among the first of the man-made varieties, and it is thought that they evolved from Silver Tabbies. They appeared first in the class for Silver Tabbies including Blue Tabbies, with or without 'white' but at the Crystal Palace show in 1894 they had their own class. These first Chinchillas were said to have resulted from Silver Tabby crosses with Blues. Apparently the early Chinchillas had silver undercoats but the tipping was slate blue. The recognized standard now says that the undercoat should be pure white, with the hairs on the back, flanks, head and ears and tail being tipped with black giving a sparkling appearance. Heavy tipping is a bad fault, as are any yellow

Chinchilla

or brown tinges in the coat. Bars too are a decided fault, as is a pale nose leather, which should be brick-red. The eyes should be emerald or blue-green.

A newly-born kitten often shows tabby markings with rings on the tail, but these should fade as the kitten develops. It is sometimes thought because of their ethereal appearance that these cats are delicate. This is not so as their stamina and hardiness equal those of any longhaired variety.

Grooming is most important and will make the fur stand up and show the tippings to the best advantage. The tail especially needs careful attention, for if any grease is allowed to accumulate at the base the hair may become dark and discoloured.

The darker-coated kittens which appear from time to time in Chinchilla litters are registered as Shaded Silvers (breed number 55). The standard for these, together with points awards, are almost the same as for the Chinchillas but the tippings are much heavier and should take the form of a mantle. The tippings can be one-third of the complete hair length but must be as even as possible. Hair on the foot pad to the joint may be shaded or black. Nose leather must be black, paw pads black or seal.

Shaded Silver

STANDARD (with scale of points)

Colour
The undercoat should be pure white, the coat on back, flanks, head, ears and tail being tipped with black, this tipping to be evenly distributed, giving the characteristic sparkling silver appearance; the legs may be very slightly shaded with the tipping, but the chin, ear tufts, stomach and chest must be pure white: any tabby marking or brown or cream tinge is a drawback. The tip of the nose should be brick-red, and the visible skin on eyelids and the pads should be black or dark brown.　25 points

Head
Broad and round, with breadth between ears and wide at the muzzle; snub nose; small well tufted ears.　20 points

Shape
Cobby with short thick legs.　15 points

Eyes
Large, round and most expressive, emerald or blue-green in colour.　15 points

Coat
Silky and fine in texture, long and dense, extra long on frill.　15 points

Tail
Short and bushy.　10 points

Golden Persian kitten

GOLDEN PERSIAN 54

This variety has been bred in the USA for many years, and a few years ago suddenly appeared in a litter here from usual Chinchillas. When the kittens were first seen, they were thought to be tabbies. This was very puzzling as it was known here was no possibility of a mis-mating. As the kittens' coats cleared it was realised that their golden coats were tipped, and the eyes were changing to green as for the Chinchillas. A number of fanciers became interested in breeding them. They became known as Golden Persians and now have champion status.

STANDARD (with scale of points)

Colour   The undercoat apricot deepening to gold. Chin, ear-tufts, stomach and chest pale apricot, rims of eyes, lips and nose outlined with seal brown or black. Back, flanks, head and tail any shade of gold sufficiently tipped with seal brown or black to give a golden appearance; the general tipping effect to be much darker than that of the usual Chinchilla.   30 points

Coat	Long and dense, and of silky texture, extra long on frill. 15 points
Head	Broad and round with breadth between the ears, which should be small and well tufted; wide at the muzzle; snub nose. 20 points
Body	Cobby with thick short legs. The legs may be shaded; back of legs from paw to heel solid colour of seal brown or black. 10 points
Nose	Brick red leather. points included with head
Paw pads	Seal brown or black. points included with body
Eyes	Large and round; green or blue-green. 15 points
Tail	Short and bushy; tipping on tail will be heavier than on the body. 10 points
Note	Golden kittens often show tabby markings and may be of unsound colour.
	Barring in adults on body or legs is a fault.

PEWTER LONGHAIR 53

The Pewter has been produced by breeding Chinchillas to Blue or Black longhairs. The colour should be white, with shadings that give the effect of a pewter mantle. The undercoat should be white, as should the ear tufts and stomach. The type and general characteristics should be as for other long-hairs. The eyes should be large and round with back rims.

STANDARD (with scale of points)

Coat	Long and dense, silky in texture with a long full frill. 10 points
Head	Broad and round with good width between the small, well tufted ears. Snub nose with nose leather brick red in colour. Firm chin and level bite. 25 points

Eyes	Orange or copper with black rims. Large and round with a pleasing expression. 10 points
Body	Cobby on short firm legs. 15 points
Tail	Short with a full brush 10 points
Colour	White, with dark tipping, giving an overall effect of a pewter mantle. 30 points

Tortoiseshell longhair

TORTOISESHELL LONGHAIR 11

This variety is considered by many to be the most fascinating of all cats with its patched coat of red, cream and black. It is virtually a female-only variety; males have been born from time to time, but do not sire. In the United States, one or two Tortie males are said to have sired, but without seeing them it is difficult to know whether they had some tabby markings and were therefore not true Torties. There is no truth in the statement that a male Tortie would be worth his weight in gold.

The variety has very little proven history, produced as they were by luck more than anything else. Those seen at the early shows were mostly of unknown parentage.

Ideally the Tortoiseshell should have a coat of bright red and cream patches, interspersed with black. The colours should be in separate patches spread all over the body, including the face, ears, legs, paws, tail and under the stomach. The patching must not be too large and should be of clear colours without white hairs or brindling. A cream or red mark known as a blaze, running down from the forehead to the nose, is liked, and does add character to the face. Large wide-open copper or deep orange eyes set well apart are desired. The type for this variety is usually very good.

Breeding Torties is still not easy. While many studs are tried, usually self-colours – Black, Cream or Red – and also Bi-colours, it is still a comparatively rare pedigree variety, although very much liked.

Faults that appear are brindling, white hairs, tabby markings and over-large patches. Intelligent, lovable, lively cats, they make good mothers and also are excellent mousers.

STANDARD (with scale of points)

Coat	Long and flowing, extra long on frill and bush. Fine of texture with the black, red and cream well broken into patches.	40 points
Body	Cobby and massive with short legs. A broad deep chest. Short and bushy tail.	20 points
Head	Round and broad; small well-placed and well-tufted ears; short broad nose, full cheeks.	25 points
Eyes	Large, full and round, deep orange or copper, brilliant in colour and set wide apart. Bold and not deep set.	15 points

It is also possible to have Chocolate Tortoiseshells (breed number 11lb) with chocolate well broken by shades of red throughout (see page 67).

TORTOISESHELL-AND-WHITE LONGHAIR 121

A most attractive female-only variety closely allied to the
Tortoiseshell, but with the addition of white to the red, cream
and black. Once referred to as the Chintz cat in Britain and
known as the Calico cat in North America, it is a very popular
and particularly striking variety. As there are effectively no
males the practice has been to use one of the self-coloured
longhaired studs, not always successfully, but any kittens
born are certainly varied and most appealing.

More recently in Britain, due to one breeder's careful study
of pedigrees and her efforts to breed Tortie-and-whites to
order, more have been seen at the shows. By mating the
Tortie-and-whites with bi-colour studs that were produced
from Tortie-and-whites, she has managed to breed a number
of kittens with good colouring and type. The studs used have
been Red-and-whites or Black-and-whites.

The colourings should spread over the body like a mantle,
interspersed with white. Too much white is a fault, but it
must be seen on the face, legs and feet, with a large amount
on the chest. Each patch must be of its own clear colour,
without brindling. Tabby markings, bars and rings are faults,
and the patching must be free of white hairs. Too little white
is also a fault. A white blaze on the forehead is much liked

Blue-tortoiseshell-and-white

and certainly adds charm to the face. The shades of the three colours and white may vary in density, producing very attractive dilutions. These are known as the Blue-tortoiseshell-and-white (breed number 12 2). There are now also further recognized varieties, as follows: Chocolate Tortie-and-white (12 3) – base colour chocolate with shades of red; Lilac Tortie-and-white (12 4) – base colour lilac and cream.

A cobby cat with a full well-covered coat and a short wide well-furnished tail is lovely to see, and Tortie-and-whites are always in great demand. The variety has been brought out for Best in Show and has won the award on several occasions.

The standard set for the Tortie-and-white is as for the Tortoiseshell Longhair, as are the awarded points.

A new group has recently been added, the Tortie Tabby-and-white, which must show both the elements of tabby and tortoiseshell, and they are as follows: Tortie Tabby-and-white (breed number 12a6t) – base colour brown tabby which has been patched and overlaid with shades of red; Blue Tortie Tabby-and-white (breed number 12a8t) – base colour blue tabby with shades of cream; Chocolate Tortie Tabby-and-white (breed number 12a9t) – base colour chocolate tabby with shades of red; Lilac Tortie Tabby-and-white (breed number 12a10t) – base colour lilac tabby with shades of cream.

BI-COLOUR LONGHAIR 12a

Cats with two-coloured coats were among the exhibits at the early cat shows, but the Black-and-whites in those days were referred to as Magpies. Harrison Weir in his book, written in 1889, gave a list of all the colours that could combine with white in such cats, but these were shorthairs and there is no reference to any longhairs. They were shown in the Any Other Colour class, and could be Black-and-white, Blue-and-white, Orange-and-white, and Tabby-and-white. In the United States the Orange-and-whites and the Blue-and-whites were given their own classification at the early shows.

Bi-colours have been bred in Britain for many years, but although liked, were considered of little interest for breeding, so the kittens were sold as pets and usually neutered. One breeder, however, realized that by careful selective breeding these cats would be most useful in the breeding of the ever elusive Tortoiseshell-and-whites. In 1966 they were granted recognition, but the required standard, based on the markings of that of the Dutch rabbit called for such definite colour divisions that it proved impossible to produce a cat with such exact markings. Judges were therefore withholding the challenge certificates, with the result that breeders almost gave up exhibiting the variety. In 1971 the standard was altered, specifying 'not more than two thirds of the cat's coat to be colour and not more than a half to be white'. Any colour with white is allowed. This has helped the breeders considerably and more are now being shown; several have become champions.

A Bi-colour may be mated to a Bi-colour, but to keep the type, an occasional self-coloured outcross may be necessary. This may produce some self-coloured kittens in future litters.

Bi-colours should have the same type as for other longhairs, and the mixed breeding has produced some strong healthy animals; The males are beautiful large cats. The full long flowing fur should show definite divisions of colour, and the areas of solid colour should be quite distinct. White hairs in the self-colour are a definite fault.

The standard for a Bi-coloured – any solid colour or tabby (except silver) and white; the patches of colour to be distinct without scattered white hairs. Not less than one-third and not more than half the coat to be white. Face to be patched with colour and white. Otherwise the basic standard is as for the Tortoiseshell Longhair, as are the points awarded.

Accepted varieties are Black-and-white Bi-colour (breed number 12a1), Blue-and white Bi-colour (breed number 12a2), Chocolate-and-white Bi-colour (breed number 12a3), Lilac-and-white Bi-colour (breed number 12a4), Red-and-white Bi-colour (breed number 12a5), Cream-and white Bi-colour (breed number 12a7). There are also Bi-colour tabby colours and white (12alt–12a7t). All have preliminary standards. In addition, there are Van Distributed Bi-colours and Tri-colours (12a1w–12a7w) and (12 1w–12 4w). Again all preliminary. For these the coat should be basically white with the colour confined to the head, ears and tail.

Blue, Blue-cream and Cream kittens

BLUE-CREAM LONGHAIR 13

This very popular variety is a product of matings between Blue and Cream longhairs, and occasionally the result of a Tortoiseshell mating with a Blue or even a Black longhair. It is very useful in the breeding of Creams. A shot-silk or misty haze is the desired effect, with a coat of soft and good texture of blue and cream intermingled. This is the standard aimed at in Britain and on the Continent, but in the United States the coat must be patched as in the Tortoiseshell. For many years the English Blue-creams were patched, but this was not liked, and much work was done by British breeders to get the desired intermingling and the soft texture of the hair. The two colours should be of the palest pastel shades, with no trace of red. It is often found that an almost perfect specimen has small patches of cream or blue or both on the legs, face or head. This is a fault that fanciers are endeavouring to breed out, in order to get perfect intermingling all over.

The head and body type of this breed has steadily improved, and it would be difficult to find a more cobby cat, equalling the finest specimens of the Blues and the Creams.

Males of this variety are seen very rarely and if they live are invariably sterile. There is always an element of surprise in the breeding of Blue-creams, and beginners interested in these cats may like to know that to produce a Blue-cream, a Cream female should be mated to a Blue male. This will give Cream male kittens and Blue-cream females. A Blue-cream female mated to a Cream will produce Blue-cream females, Blue males and both male and female Cream kittens. Owners of Blue females who wish to start breeding Creams should mate the Blue female to a Cream male, which will give Blue males and Blue-cream females. A Blue-cream from this cross when mated to a Cream should produce Cream males and females, Blue-cream females and Blue males. When selecting a kitten from one of these matings, the one which appears to have no markings or patches and has the palest coat should be chosen as being most likely to produce that most elusive perfectly intermingled Blue-cream. Lilac-creams (breed number 11c) are now being bred with the pastel shades of lilac and cream softly intermingled throughout the coat to the extremities.

STANDARD

Head and Ears	Head round and massive with great breadth of skull; well balanced. Small round-tipped ears set wide apart and low on the head, fitting into the rounded contour of the skull, with full ear furnishings but not unduly open at the base. Full cheeks; round forehead. Short broad nose of even width with stop (break). Nose leather fully formed. Strong chin and full muzzle with broad, powerful jaws, without a 'pinch'. Short thick neck.
Eyes	Large, full, round eyes; deep orange or copper, brilliant in colour and set well apart.
Body	Large or medium cobby type, with deep chest, massive shoulders and rump.
Legs and Paws	Short, thick, strong legs, Large, round, firm paws, perfectly well tufted. Toes carried close.
Tail	Short and bushy, but in proportion to the body length.
Coat	Long and thick. Fine in texture, soft and full of life.

52

COLOURPOINT 13b (1–20)

The colourpoint was first granted recognition by the Governing Council of the Cat Fancy in 1955, but some eight years of selective intensive breeding before that date had been necessary to produce the desired results.

At the same time, unknown to the British breeders, similar cats were being developed in the United States where they were recognized in 1957 and given the name of Himalayan. Colourpoints have turned up as a result of chance matings among domestic cats but the fine specimens we have today did not originate in this manner. The object of Colourpoint breeding was to produce a cat of true Persian type but with the coat pattern and eye colour of the Siamese. It is not in any way a longhaired Siamese as some may imagine.

When a longhaired cat is mated with a Siamese it does not produce a Colourpoint, such a mating produces shorthaired self-coloured kittens. Each of these kittens is carrier of the genes for both the long hair and the Siamese coat pattern. These carriers mated together would on average produce only one kitten in thirty-two showing the Siamese coat pattern, blue eyes and long hair, but it would not possess the Persian type. To achieve this was a slow process and required the introduction into the breeding line of the finest type

Colourpoint: Blue-point

longhairs available, and many such matings had to take place before the true longhair type became established.

Gradually over the years the Colourpoints have improved until today many are very close to the standard laid down by the Governing Council which requires them to have round broad heads, with good width between the small ears. The fur should be long and silky and the face framed by a full ruff. Serious faults are kinked tails, and more recently as the type has improved, the exaggerated undershot jaw.

Today most of the best Colourpoints are produced by selective breeding, mating Colourpoint to Colourpoint and using only the best from each generation for future breeding. The early Colourpoints were all Seal-points or Blue-points; the Seal-point has a cream body colour and the Blue-point has glacial white.

One difficulty with the Seals and Blues is that unfortunately the body colouring does tend to darken on the shoulders and flanks after the second year. In some instances the overall colour darkens as the cat grows older, and the body fur becomes brindled, taking on a 'badger' appearance.

With a simple knowledge of genetics and planned breeding, it is possible to produce Colourpoints in any colouring desired

Colourpoint: Red-point

and in fact there are now many other colour variations. The
first to appear after the Seals and Blues were the Lilac-points.
These were bred not only for their beauty but because it was
thought, quite correctly, that they would retain their pale
coats throughout life. Once again it was necessary to use a
Siamese, or a self-coloured chocolate shorthair to introduce
the chocolate or brown gene.

Thus a Chocolate-point Siamese was mated with a Seal-
point Colourpoint (carrying blue). This produced offspring of
poor type, but in an interesting range of variety, both
shorthaired and longhaired, and of four different point
colours. To get from this stage to Chocolate-point and Lilac-
point Colourpoints of good type, it was necessary to
crossbreed with outstanding longhairs, and this proved a
long slow process. However it was successfully done and the
results may be seen and admired at the shows; several have
already gained championships.

There are now also Red-, Cream-, Tortoiseshell- and Blue-
cream-points, the latter two being female-only varieties. To
produce these four it was not necessary to use any shorthaired
cats, as there are many excellent Cream and Red longhairs
available for the introduction of the gene for yellow or red.

Colourpoint : Blue-cream-point

However, this gene is inherited in a slightly different way as it is borne by one of the sex chromosomes (sex linked). As a result at least three generations are needed to produce litters with both sexes of Red-or Cream-point. Once obtained these cats breed true, that is, all the offspring are the colours required. Usually they have a wealth of almost white coat, but the points do not reach their full depth of colour until the second year.

The most recent colour varieties to be produced are the Tabby-point and Tortie Tabby-point, and they are the most spectacular; the tabby markings show up clearly on the face, with the 'M' mark on the forehead and the black pencillings, like spectacles, around the large blue eyes.

TABBY-POINT STANDARD

The basic standard and the scale of points is as described on page 57 for the Colourpoint.

Coat   There should be a clearly defined 'M' marking on the forehead, 'spectacle' markings round the eyes and spotted whisker pads. The front legs have broken rings from the toes upwards; barring on the hind legs is confined to the front of the upper leg and the thigh, the back of the leg from the toe to hock being solid points colours. Ears solid and not clearly showing 'thumb marks' which are less apparent in dilute colours and mottled in the Tortie Tabby-points. Hair inside the ears lighter, giving the appearance of a pale rim, ears tufts lighter in colour. Tail with broken rings.

Head	Round and massive with great breadth of skull. Full cheeks, round forehead. Nose leather pinkish outline in pigment, or to tone with the points. Eye rims and paw pads to tone in with the points.
Eyes	Large, round and full Clear, bright and decidedly blue. The lids to be dark rimmed or toning with the points.
Body	Cobby and low on leg.
Tail	Short and full, not tapering. A kink shall be considered a defect.
Faults	Any similarity in type to Siamese to be considered undesirable and incorrect.

A Colourpoint in full coat and in perfect condition is undoubtedly one of the most beautiful of the longhairs and Colourpoints have become immensely popular both on the show bench and as pets. Their temperament is less boisterous and demanding than that of the Siamese. Gentle and affectionate, each has an individual personality and inquiring nature, following their owners around the house in an almost doglike fashion.

STANDARD (with scale of points)

Coat	Including colour, texture and quality; points for eveness of colour, tabby markings, patching and intermingling as appropriate. 25 points

The colour varieties are as follows:

57

Seal-point—creamy-white body colour, seal brown points. 13b1

Blue-point—glacial white body colour, blue points. 13b2

Chocolate-point—ivory-white with chocolate points. 13b3

Lilac-point—magnolia-white with lilac points. 13b4

Red-point—apricot-white with rich red points. 13b5

Seal Tortie-point—cream with seal and red points. 13b6

Cream-point—creamy-white with cream toning points. 13b7

Blue Cream-point—glacial to creamy-white with blue and cream points. 13b8

Lilac Cream-point—magnolia to creamy-white with lilac and cream points. 13b9

Chocolate Tortie-point—ivory to apricot white with chocolate and red points. 13b10

Tabby point colours follow the above breeds 13b1–13b5 and 13b7. 13b11–13b15 and 13b17 Tortie-tabby point colours follow the above breeds 13b6 and 13b8–13b10.

13b16 and 13b18-13b20

Head	Including general head shape and set of eyes, nose length, width and stop. 30 points
Eyes	Including size (large), shape (round and full) and colour (decidedly blue). 20 points
Body	Including shape (cobby), size and bone structure; tail and length of tail (short and bushy), height, and thickness of leg. 25 points
Note	Any similarity in type to Siamese, in particular a long straight nose, to be considered most undesirable and incorrect.

BIRMAN 13c (1–20)

This attractive variety has been exhibited since 1951 in France, where it is known as the Sacred Cat of Burma. There is a legend that the cats were originally white, and centuries ago were kept in the temples of Burma. One cat named Sinh was kept as an oracle by the high priest in a temple. At that time the country was seriously threatened by enemies, and the high priest, worn out with concern for his country, died suddenly in the temple.

In a miracle of transmigration Sinh changed from white to a golden colour, his eyes from yellow to sapphire blue, and his feet, tail and ears dark brown like the earth. The tips of his paws, having touched the head of his master, remained white. On seeing this miracle the other priests found the courage to go and repel the invaders, and this they did.

Sinh stayed by the body for seven days, refusing all food until he died, carrying his master's soul to paradise. When the priests assembled to choose a new leader the hundred temple cats came in and they were no longer white but had taken on the same colouring as the dead Sinh. They surrounded the youngest of the priests, and so he was chosen.

Birman kitten

Ever since then the Birmans have had the same colouring as the temple cats and Sinh.

They are an unusual variety, with the Siamese coat pattern and long, slightly golden fur on the body; they have contrasting points, and the added and distinctive attraction of four white gloved paws.

Unknown in Britain until 1964–65 when two breeders imported the first pair seen here, they were at first exhibited in the Any Other Variety classes. Then, as they proved to breed true they were granted recognition in 1966. Among the first champions in Britain were Paranjoti Chimea and Paranjoti Katmandu. Other imports have followed from both France and Germany, where Birmans are also bred, and Birmans from Britain are now exported all over the world.

The Birmans differ from most longhairs in being longer in the body, rather than cobby, with heads not so broad (but not at all like that of the Siamese) and longish bushy tails. The eyes are bright blue. The front paws should have the pure white gloves ending in an even line across the paw, and the back paws pure white gloves, usually referred to as gauntlets, should cover the entire paw and taper up the back of the leg finishing in a point. It is essential that the front paws should match, as also should the back gauntlets.

In the Seal-point Birmans the body is a clear pale beige, slightly golden, with dark brown points, and in the Blue-point Birmans the body fur is bluish white, rather cold in tone, with blue-grey points. There are also Chocolate, Lilac, Red and Cream-point Birmans (breed numbers 13c3, 4, 5, and 7 respectively); additionally there are Tabby-point Birmans which have the same colour range as the solid points (breed numbers 13c11–17 excluding 16), together with Seal Tortie-points (breed numbers 13c6–10) and Tortie Tabby-points (breed numbers 13c16–20) but for neither of these are there red or cream varieties.

STANDARD (with scale of points)

Body	Long and massive with thickset legs of medium length. Paws short and strong. Pad colour irrelevant. 20 points
Head	Broad and round, nose of medium length, no stop, cheeks full, ears medium-sized, spaced well apart. 20 points
Eyes	Blue, the deeper the better, almost round. 15 points
Tail	Bushy, medium in length. 5 points
Coat	Long with full ruff, silky in texture with distinguishing colours as those for the Siamese (see pages 138–148). Mask, ears, legs and tail clearly defined. 20 points
Paws	Front paws always have pure white symmetrical gloves ending in an even line across the paw and not passing beyond the angle formed by the paw and leg. Back paws have pure white gloves (gauntlets) covering the entire paw and tapering up the back of the leg. The white feet are characteristic of the Birman. 20 points

It is important that when the cat is well grown, the frame (skeleton) should be strong, well-covered and muscular. Eyes bright, temperament good.

TURKISH VAN 13d

There are many kinds of cat in Turkey, all of different colours and with all lengths of fur. The first longhairs seen in Europe were the Angoras, all white cats; a very similar variety to this, known as the Turkish Angora, is now bred in the United States and is just beginning to be bred in Britain.

Another variety, which has come direct from Turkey into Britain is simply called the Turkish Van. It was introduced in 1956 by two British breeders who first encountered the variety in the area of Lake Van in Turkey and were struck by its unusual appearance. An unrelated pair were imported into England, and they proved to breed true. Other imports followed, but owing to the difficulty of finding, suitable pairs and the time and cost of quarantine their development has been slow, and it was not until 1969 that the standard was approved and championship status granted.

The Turkish cats have long chalk-white fur and auburn markings on the faces, with full auburn tails. The head is wedge-shaped, but shorter and not so extreme as that of the Siamese; the light amber coloured eyes are pink rimmed. Some cats do have auburn markings on other parts of the body but this does not mean disqualification.

Young Turkish Van kittens

Although it is commonly supposed that cats dislike water, these cats and even young kittens are said to enjoy swimming both in fast-running streams and still water in Turkey, and those bred in Britain love to play with water. Probably because of the extreme climate in the country of origin, the Turkish cats lose most of their coats in the summer, looking almost short coated, but the fur grows again very quickly as winter approaches.

The litters average four; the newly-born kittens show auburn markings clearly in the white fur. Highly intelligent, they make delightful pets.

They have been exported all over the world from Britain but unfortunately the numbers seen at the shows here have increased very little.

STANDARD (with scale of points)

Colour and coat	Chalk white with no trace of yellow. Auburn markings on face with white blaze. Ears white; nose tip, pads and inside ears a delicate shell pink. Fur long, soft and silky to the roots; no woolly undercoat. 25 points

63

Head	Short wedge; nose long. Eyes large and oval with pink rims.	25 points
Ears	Large, well-feathered, fairly close together and set high on head.	10 points
Eyes	For colour only; must be appropriate.	5 points
Body	Long and sturdy with full bushy tail. Legs medium in length. Feet neat, well-rounded and tufted.	25 points
Condition	Well groomed with no trace of grease, staining or tangles.	5 points

The Auburn Turkish Van (breed number 13d) as described on page 62 has light amber eyes. There is also a blue-eyed (13dbl) and odd-eyed (one blue and one light amber) 13dod). There are also three varieties of Cream Turkish Van (breed number 13df), including the blue-eyed and odd-eyed.

Chocolate longhair

RECENTLY RECOGNIZED BREEDS

In recent years may new varieties have been recognized and these continue to gain in popularity.

CHOCOLATE LONGHAIR 50b

Although breeding for chocolates was started many years ago, it was only recently given a standard of points. The variety was produced in the first place through Colourpoint breeding, and it has taken many years of careful selective breeding to produce coats of an even chocolate colour, and good type. Previously the noses have been a little too long and the ears rather tall; the eye colour was not always the desired deep orange or copper. They now have championship status and so another 'man-made' variety has been established.

STANDARD

The basic standard and the scale of points is as described on page 18 for the Persian Black Self Longhair.

Colour   Medium to dark chocolate, warm in tone and sound and even in colour, free from shading, markings or white hairs. Nose leather, eye rims and paw pads chocolate.

Eyes   Copper or deep orange.

NORWEGIAN FOREST 67

Semi-longhaired cats, with quick-drying double coats that are well suited to the harsh Scandinavian winters. The head is triangular, with high-set open ears. Strongly-built with long legs; tail should be long and bushy, eyes large, well opened and slightly oblique. All eye colours allowed regardless of coat colour. All colours and cost patterns are allowed except chocolate, lilac and Siamese pattern (see photograph on page 8).

LILAC LONGHAIR 50c

The Lilac colouring is a dilute form of the brown colouring of the Chocolate variety, and has been created by careful breeding on much the same lines. The colour should be a pinkish dove grey and this has been very difficult to produce accurately. There has been a great improvement, but the numbers seen are still very low. The type should be as for the other longhairs.

STANDARD

The basic standard and the scale of points is described on page 18 for the Persian Black Self Longhair.

Colour   Lilac, warm in tone and sound and even in colour, free from shading, markings or white hairs. Nose leather, eye rims and paw pads lilac. (Incorrect pigment in these areas is a fault, for which certificates will be withheld.)

Eyes   Copper or deep orange.

Tail   Short and full, not tapering. A kink is a fault.

LILAC-CREAM LONGHAIR AND
CHOCOLATE-TORTOISESHELL LONGHAIR

These are two of the newest longhaired varieties, which now
have provisional standards. Produced by further selective
breeding and with the introduction of cream, the Lilac-cream
should have a softly intermingled coat, as that required for
the Blue-cream. The eyes should be copper, and the type as
for other longhairs.

The Chocolate-tortoiseshell should have a well patched
coat of chocolate, red and cream, similar to that of the
Tortoiseshell. The patching should be distinct and the colours
bright. The eyes may be deep orange or copper.

STANDARD

The basic standard and the scale of points is as described on
page 46 for the Tortoiseshell.

TIFFANIE   68

A cat of the Asian group which is the name for cats of
Burmese type of non-Burmese coat colour, pattern or
length. The Tiffanie should have a semi-long coat, silky and
fine in texture with the fur noticeably longer on the tail.
There should be a distinct ruff round the neck. The
furnishings from inside the ears should form 'streamers' and
tufts at the tips of the ears are acceptable. The coat may be
black, blue, chocolate, lilac, red, caramel tortie, or the
Burmese colour restriction of any of these colours or their
silver varieties, in any of the recognized Asian patterns. The
overall type should be similar to the Burmese cat. A
tendency to Siamese type or cobbiness is not permissible.

Cinnamon and lilac Angoras

ANGORA 62

The first longhairs in Europe were Angoras, named after the city now called Ankara. Because the Persian type came to be preferred the Angoras virtually died out in the West. Recently however, interest in the Angoras has revived in America and breeding has started there once again, these cats are called Turkish Angoras. Angoras are also being bred in Britain once more, but in all the colours and patterns of pedigree longhairs, while the original Angoras were mostly white.

The heads are wedge-shaped, the bodies long and lithe, and the tails long and thin. The ears are large and the eye colour should be in keeping with the coat colouring. The fur length is not so profuse as that of other longhairs.

Angoras are not to be confused with the variety known as Turkish cats, described on page 62.

The very extensive Angora family includes self colours, tortoiseshells, smokes, shaded, tabby and tortie tabby coats, with 20 points awarded for coat length and condition and a further 20 points for colour and pattern. Preliminary standard is similar to that of the Balinese.

CAMEOS   51,52

The cameo factor was obtained by mating a silver to a red gened cat, or its dilute form, cream; the cats are similar to the Chinchilla, Smoke and Shaded Silver, with red tipping instead of black. The undercoat should be white, and the type and general characteristics as for other longhairs.

The Shell Cameo is comparable to the Chinchilla in the length of tipping, giving a rose coloured haze, while the Shaded Cameo has tippings similar to those of the Shaded Silver, giving the effect of a sparkling red mantle. The frill, ear tufts, and undercoat are white.

The Tortie Cameo in the Red Series and the Blue-Cream Cameo in the Cream Series are female-only varieties, very useful in breeding.

Red Series   *51*

A Cameo is a cat of contrasts, the undercoat being as white as possible, with the tips shading to red or tortoiseshell. The deepest intensity of colour being most defined on mask, along the spine from head to tip of tail, and on legs and feet; the light points on frill, flanks, undersurfaces and ear tufts.

Coat   Coat long and dense, silky and fine in texture,
            extra long frill.   10 points

Head   Broad and round with snub nose, good width
            between small well tufted ears. Firm chin and
            level bite.   25 points

Eyes   Deep, orange or copper, large and round with a
            pleasing expression. A green rim to the eye
            considered a fault.   10 points

Body and legs Cobby, not coarse but massive, well coupled
            with short firm legs.   15 points

Tail   Short and bushy. A kink to be considered a
            defect.   10 points

Colour   **51(1) Shell**   Characteristic sparkling silver
            appearance, lightly dusted with rose pink. Nose
            leather and pads pink.

            51(2) Shaded   White evenly shaded with red
            giving the overall effect of a red mantle. Nose
            leather and pads pink. Tabby markings undesir-
            able.

            51(4) Tortie Cameo   Tipping to comprise
            black, red and cream, broken into patches. Colours
            to be rich and bright, well broken into patches
            on the face. Tippings of any intensity acceptable.
            Solid colours on legs and feet undesirable. Nose
            leather black, pink or a combination of the two.
                    The coat colour is awarded 30 points.

Cameo kitten

Cream Series   52

The previous page is also the standard for the Cream Series, except that where the word 'red' occurs, 'cream' should be substituted.

STANDARD

Colour   **52(1) Shell**   Characteristic sparkling silver appearance, lightly dusted with cream. Nose leather and pads pink.

52(2) Shaded   White evenly shaded with cream giving the overall effect of a cream mantle. Nose leather and pads pink. Tabby markings undesirable.

52(4) Blue Cream Cameo   Tipping to consist of blue and cream softly intermingled. Tipping of any intensity acceptable. Nose leather blue, pink or combination of the two.

Balinese : red-pointed

BALINESE

Known for some years in the United States and other countries, the Balinese are now being bred in Britain. They are long dainty cats, with wedge-shaped heads, large pointed ears and almond shaped eyes of vivid blue. The fine and silky fur is not as long as that of most other longhaired varieties, and the fur may have a tendency to wave where it is longest. The tail is long, thin and tapering, and should be well covered with silky fur.

Although they have the Siamese coat pattern, light body colouring with the contrasting points, and the longer fur there is no similarity between them and the Colourpoints, which have a definite longhair type.

STANDARD (with scale of points)

The Balinese cat should be a beautifully balanced animal, with head, ears and neck carried on a lithe and graceful body, supported on slim legs and feet, with tail in proportion. The head and profile should be wedge shaped, neither round nor pointed. The mask complete, connected by tracings with the ears (except in kittens), the eyes a clear bright blue, expression alert and intelligent.

The award of points is split between those for type (50 points) and those for colour and coat (50 points).

Body	Medium size, lithe and graceful.	15 points
Head	Long and well-proportioned.	15 points
Ears	Rather large and pricked.	5 points
Eyes	Oriental in shape and slanted.	5 points
Legs	Proportionally slim with hind legs slightly higher than front legs. Feet small and oval.	5 points
Tail	Long and tapering, free from kink.	5 points
Coat	Medium long, fine and silky in texture, without woolly undercoat, lying mainly flat along the body; tail plume-like.	15 points
Eye colour	Bright clear blue, and complementary to points colour.	15 points
Points colour	Mask, ears, legs, feet and tail clearly defined, dense with colour, matching in tone on all points.	10 points
Body colour	As individual colour standards, with clear contrast between points and body colour; length of coat may affect depth of tone.	10 points

The recognized Balinese coat patterns are the Seal-point (breed number 61) and Blue, Lilac, Chocolate, Cream, Red and Tabby-points and Tortie-points of all the above with the exception of Red.

SOMALI 63

Now established on the show bench are the Somalis, cats with Abyssinian type and colourings, but with medium length soft silky fur having the typical banded ticking. Very gentle friendly cats, with beautiful large almond shaped eyes, they are proving very popular. The colours are as for the Abyssinians, that is Usual, with coat a rich golden brown

Somali

ticked with black, with the underside of the body a rich apricot tone and the Sorrel with fur a warm glowing copper ticked with cinnamon, with base hair deep apricot, and the ears and tail tipped with cinnamon. Chocolate, Blue, Lilac, Fawn, Red and Cream are the other colours. All of the above colours can also be in Silver (for example Sorrel Silver, breed number 63as), for which base hair should be silvery white. All colours, except Red and Cream, also appear as Tortie Somalis and Tortie Silver Somalis, which brings the family range to 28 different coats.

The overall impression of the Somali is that of a well-proportioned, medium-sized cat of foreign type, with coat of medium length, and firm, muscular development, lithe, showing an alert, lively interest in all surroundings, with an even disposition and easy to handle. The cat should have a well-balanced appearance of activity, sound health and general vigour with a good weight for its size.

STANDARD *(with scale of points)*

Head   A moderate wedge, the brow, cheek and profile lines all showing a gentle contour. A slight rise from the bridge of the nose to the forehead, which should be of good size with width between the ears, flowing into the arched neck without a break. A shallow indentation forming the muzzle is desirable, but a pinch is a fault. In profile the head shows a gentle rounding to the brow, a slight nose break is essential, leading to a firm chin. The muzzle shall not be sharply pointed and there shall be no evidence of snipiness or whisker pinch.   15 points

Ears   Ears set wide apart and pricked, broad at base, pricked, well cupped and tufted.   10 points

Eyes   Almond shaped, set well apart, large, brilliant and expressive. Skull aperture neither round nor oriental. Eyes accentuated by dark lid-skin, encircled by light coloured 'spectacles'. Above each eye a short dark vertical 'pencil' stroke with a dark 'pencil' line continuing from the upper lid towards the ear.   10 points

Legs and feet   Legs in proportion to torso, feet oval and tufted between the toes.   5 points

Tail   Slightly tapering. Its length to balance with the torso.   10 points

Coat   The texture is very soft to the touch, extremely fine, dense and double coated with at least 3 bands of ticking which is the essence of the Somali coat. The coat is of a medium length, except over the shoulders, where a shorter length is permitted. A full-coated appearance is preferred. Points are awarded for the coat as follows: colour, 10; ticking, 15; texture, 5; length, 10; total   40 points

Disqualify White locket or white patch, or white anywhere on body other than in the area of the chin, lips and nostrils, and stemming from lower jaw; any skeletal abnormality, wrong colour paw pads or nose leather, incorrect number of toes, kinks in tail.

Maine Coon

MAINE COON   64

This very old American variety is now making its appearance in Britain. Produced in the first place in Maine, USA by matings between the resident domestic shorthairs and cats with long coat brought by travellers in the middle eighties, they had individual shows as early as 1860. Large strong cats, with semi-longhair coats. Many colour combinations are accepted, but 'colour' is of far less importance than type, size and coat quality. The head is of medium length, with large tufted ears and full round eyes.

RAGDOLL   66

Another American variety imported into Britain, the Ragdoll is a large cat, so called because it is so relaxed when picked up. It is also said not to feel pain, so possible injuries should be guarded against. There are four colours: seal, blue, chocolate and lilac, which are in three patterns: colourpoint, mitted or bi-colour. The fur is long and the tail also long and full. Head is of medium size with medium-sized ears and large oval eyes.

Originally from the USA, with hair slightly longer than the other Shorthairs. Extensive colour range similar to the longhair breeds.

STANDARD (with scale of points)

Head	Round and massive with good breadth of skull, ears small, round-tipped.	30 points
Body	Large or medium in size, of cobby type, low on legs. Broad deep chest, tail short.	20 points
Coat	Dense, plush, soft in texture.	20 points
Colour	White markings anywhere a fault, unless referred to in the individual colour description.	20 points
Eyes	Large, full, round; brilliant in colour and set well apart.	10 points

Exotic shorthair

BRITISH SHORTHAIRED CATS

British cats are not just 'ordinary' house cats. They are pedigree in that they have been bred from like parents and that the like ancestors of these parents were of good pedigree and sound breeding for several generations. Shorthaired cats have been known in Britain for generations, it is thought from the time of the Romans; and for centuries they have been companions of man. They bred together and interbred, but as the stock was of strong constitution this has not impaired the stamina of their progeny. They were the common ancestors, through selective breeding for a century or more, of the splendid British cats we have today.

These intelligent and charming creatures are graceful and active, taking a great interest in everything that goes on in the house and garden. They are not so destructive to the furniture as are so many other breeds, preferring when they can to use trees in the garden to sharpen their claws. They make good show cats, seemingly unperturbed by the hustle and bustle of the shows and the change from their daily routine.

When buying a British cat it is desirable to choose one with a pedigree of three generations of like-to-like, and one that has a good broad head, with small rounded ears, and large round eyes, a sturdy body, and a short thick tail.

It is unwise to mate a British cat to a longhaired cat, for although this is done from time to time in order to keep the type, it may also breed in longish fur, rather than the short dense coat required. The fur should be short and close, firm to the touch, and of good texture.

A short coat is more easily kept in order than that of the longhaired breeds, although this does not mean that they can do without a daily grooming with the hands. Hard hand stroking tones up the muscles and takes out the old loose hair, thus allowing the new growth to come in evenly. It is unwise to use a comb too often, as this tends to open and soften the coat, but a soft brush may be used sometimes. The well-groomed cat is less liable to fur ball, that is the mass of hair which accumulates in the stomach with the cat's continual washing and grooming of itself.

There are a number of varieties of the British shorthaired cat, and the most popular is the British Blue, with the silver Tabbies and the Spotted coming second.

The type required for the British cat is the same for all varieties and is as given in the general standard.

GENERAL STANDARD

The British cat is compact, well balanced and powerful, showing good depth of body, a full broad chest, short strong legs, rounded paws, tail thick at base with rounded tip. The head is round with a good width between the ears, round cheeks, firm chin, small ears, large round and well-opened eyes and a short broad nose. The coat is short and dense.

Head	Round face with full cheeks and good breadth of skull with round underlying bone structure. The head should be set on a short thick neck.
Nose	The nose itself should be short, broad and straight. In profile, a rounded forehead should lead to a short, straight nose with a nose break which is neither too pronounced nor too shallow.
Chin	A strong, firm and deep chin is essential. Any deviation from this to be considered a fault. The bite MUST be level, the tip of the chin to line up with the tip of the nose in the same vertical plane.
Ears	Small rounded at the tips. Set far apart fitting into (without distorting) the rounded contour of the head. External ear to be well covered with fur, internal furnishings not to be excessive.
Eyes	Large, round and well-opened. Set wide apart with no tendency to oriental shape. No squint.
Body	Cobby type with short level back. Low on legs with broad deep chest. Equally massive across the shoulders and the rump. Medium to large, but not rangey.

79

Paws	Round and firm. Toes carried close, five on each forefoot (including dew-claw) and four on each back foot.
Tail	Should be thick and of medium length, thicker at the base with rounded tip.
Coat	Must be short, dense and crisp. A soft and/or over-long and fluffy coat is incorrect.
Condition	Perfect physical condition, muscular with alert appearance.

Points are awarded as follows:

	Self	**Patterned**
Head and Ears	20 points	25 points
Eyes	10 points	10 points
Body, legs and paws	25 points	20 points
Tail	10 points	5 points
Coat texture, length	20 points	–
Colour	15 points	–
Texture, length, colour and pattern		40 points

Faults are uneven coat colour, colour mark on head in Whites, heavy silver tipping in Blues, heavy tabby markings.

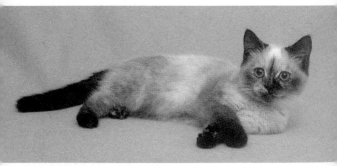

Colourpoint: newest variety of British shorthair

WHITE SHORTHAIRS   14, 14a, 14b

There are three varieties of the shorthaired Whites, with exactly the same standards except for the eye colouring. The coats should be pure white, with no trace of yellow.

The Whites are very clean cats, seeming to realise that their fur calls for constant grooming on their part to present a spotless appearance. Talcum powder may be sprinkled right down into the roots of the fur, then brushed out completely with a soft brush. Some owners bath their Whites, using a baby shampoo and rinsing out thoroughly, always avoiding the eyes and inside the ears, and drying the cat completely before allowing it outside.

The Blue-eyed White (14) should have eyes of intense sapphire. Unfortunately few are now being bred. This may be partly because of the deafness which does occur in both longhaired and shorthaired blue-eyed cats (although not in all) and also because it is difficult to produce Whites with really deep blue eyes. Some White kittens are born with a few black hairs on their heads, which usually disappear as they grow older. It is said that these kittens are rarely deaf.

White shorthair : odd-eyed

The orange-eyed variety (14a) should have really deep orange eyes, never pale yellow, while the odd-eyed variety (14b) should have one really deep blue eye and one orange.

STANDARD

The basic standard and the scale of points is as described on page 80 for the British Shorthair.

Colour	White to be pure, untinged with yellow. Pink nose leather and pads.
Eyes	Blue-eyed (14): very deep sapphire blue. No green rims or flecks. Orange-eyed (14a): gold, orange or copper. No green rims or flecks. Odd-eyed (14b): one gold, orange or copper. One blue. No green rims or flecks.
Withhold certificates	Incorrect eye colour. Green rims.

BLACK SHORTHAIR 15

Black cats are found in great numbers as household pets, but they may have green eyes and white hairs somewhere in the fur, and it is not appreciated how beautiful a black can be until one sees a pedigree British, with shining jet black coat, no signs of rustiness, and big round orange or deep copper eyes. It is a difficult task to produce a Black without a single white hair, although many conform to the standard required in every other way.

There are many superstitions connected with black cats left over from the middle ages when they were connected with witchcraft and black magic, but the cats depicted in old prints with witches are usually long and slinky, with slanting green eyes, very different in temperament and looks from the 'square' British Blacks.

STANDARD

The basic standard and the scale of points is as described on page 8o for the British Shorthair.

Colour   Jet black to the roots with no rusty tinge.

British Blue shorthair

Other self-coloured British Shorthairs are Chocolate (15b)— any shade of rich chocolate; Lilac (15c)— frosty grey with a distinct pinkish tone giving an overall lilac appearance; Red Self (15d)— deep rich red.

BRITISH BLUE (16)

The Blue is the most popular of all the British varieties; in recent years there has been a renewed interest in Blues and the kittens are in great demand both as show cats and as pets. A good specimen with a coat of even blue, no shadings, no white hairs and good copper or orange eyes is always much sought after.

In the same way that is described in the sections on the longhaired Blues, Creams and Blue-creams, the British Blue may be used to breed several shorthaired varieties.

There are few British Blues in Europe, although there are some outstanding ones in Scandinavia, and the French have a variety called the Chartreux, said to have been brought to

British Blue shorthair kitten

France from South Africa by the monks of the order of Chartreux. Some people insist that these are identical with the British Blue, but the general opinion is that there is a certain difference in that the fur is more greyish-blue, the heads are not quite so round and the chest is deeper.

STANDARD

The basic standard and the scale of points is as described on page 80 for the British Shorthair.

Colour	Light to medium blue. Even colour and no tabby markings or white anywhere. Nose leather and pads blue.
Eyes	Copper, orange or deep gold.
Faults	Unsound coats, Silver tipping to coats. Incorrect eye colour.

British Cream shorthair

CREAM SHORTHAIR 17

These charming cats are still comparatively rare, few appearing on the show bench. It is exceedingly difficult to produce this variety without shadow rings on the tail, and sometimes faint tabby markings in the coat. The standard says that lighter shades of cream are preferred, even in colour. Some, however, perhaps as a result of being Tortoiseshell bred, tend to be 'hot', that is, the colour may be too red.

Creams may be mated to Blues to produce Blues, Creams and Blue-Creams, and may be bred from Tortoiseshells. The eyes may be copper or orange, and the type is usually good.

STANDARD

The basic standard and scale of points is as described on page 80 for the British Shorthair.

Colour	Pale-toned cream, neither red nor fawn. Sound to the roots. Coat to have fewest markings possible. No white hairs. Nose leather and pads pink.
Eyes	Copper, orange or deep gold.
Faults	Incorrect eye colour. Heavy tabby markings.

Brown Classic Tabby kitten

SHORTHAIRED TABBIES   18, 19, 20

Cats with stripes were depicted by the ancient Egyptians and many domestic pets are marked in some form or another. Some of the longhaired and shorthaired self-coloured pedigree kittens have shadow tabby markings, but these usually disappear as they grow older. In spite of this, to breed a tabby with the correct pattern of markings is quite difficult.

There are three colour variations, as in the longhairs: Silver, Red and Brown. There are two pattern variations, the classic tabby and the mackerel tabby. The mackerel tabbies are, however, few and far between; their colours are exactly the same as those of the classic tabbies, and they are judged in the same classes. The type for both classic and mackerel tabbies is the same as for all British shorthairs.

PATTERN STANDARD

CLASSIC TABBY

All markings to be clearly defined and dense. Legs barred evenly with bracelets going down from the body markings to the toes. Ground colour and markings should be equally balanced. Evenly ringed tail. On the neck and upper chest there should be unbroken necklaces, the more the better. On the forehead there should be a letter 'M' made by brown marks. There should be an unbroken line running back from the outer corner of the eye. There should be pencillings on the cheeks. There should be a vertical line which runs over the back of the head and extends to the shoulder markings, which should be shaped like a butterfly. Both the upper and the lower wings should be defined clearly in outline with dots inside this outline.

On the back there should be a line running down the spine from the butterfly to the tail, and there should be a stripe on each side of this running parallel to it. These stripes should be separated from each other by stripes of the ground colour. On each flank there should be a large solid oyster or blotch which should be surrounded by one or more unbroken rings. The markings on each side should be identical. All tabby cats should be spotted in the abdominal region. In all tabby cats the tails should be evenly ringed.

PATTERN STANDARD

MACKEREL TABBY

Head, legs and tail as for Classic Tabby. There should be a narrow unbroken line running from the back of the head to the base of the tail. The rest of the body to be covered with narrow lines running vertically down from the spine line, also to be unbroken. These lines should be as narrow and as numerous as possible.

Pattern faults   Solid back, broken tail rings, solid sides, white tip to tail and white anywhere. Spotting on back. Brindling.

Withhold certificates   Incorrect eye colour. White anywhere. Incorrect mackerel pattern.

SILVER TABBY SHORTHAIR   (18)

This is probably the most popular of the shorthaired tabbies, with pure silver background colouring, without brindling, and the pattern of markings in black standing out quite

Silver Tabby Shorthair

sharply. Apart from White and Black the Silver Tabby appears in all the other self colours.

STANDARD

The basic standard and the scale of points is as described on page 80 for the British Shorthair.

Colour
Clear silver ground colour which should include chin and lips. Markings dense black. Nose leather brick red for preference, black permissible. Pads and soles of feet from toes to heel black. For markings *see* pattern standards.

Eyes
Green or hazel.

Faults
Brown on nose or paws. Brindling.

Withhold certificates
Incorrect eye colour. White anywhere.

RED TABBY SHORTHAIR (19)

The body colour of this variety must be a good deep colour, not a pale marmalade or sandy hue as seen in many pets. The markings again must be dark red, standing out quite

Red Tabby shorthair

distinctly from the background. The markings are as given in the pattern standards above, and the type is British. A cluster or star of white under the neck, on the chest or between the legs low on the belly is a serious fault, and no cat with such markings will be awarded a challenge certificate. A white tip to the tail is also a fault.

As is the case for the Red Longhair, Red Tabbies are not necessarily all males (*see* p. 26). When the parentage is pure Red Tabby both females and males may be in the litter.

STANDARD

The basic standard and the scale of points is as described on page 80 for the British Shorthair.

Colour	Red ground colour and markings of deep rich red. Lips and chin red, nose leather brick red; pads deep red, sides of feet dark red. For markings *see* pattern standards.
Eyes	Brilliant orange or deep copper.
Faults	Brindling or uneven ground colour.
Withhold certificates	Incorrect eye colour. White anywhere.

BROWN TABBY SHORTHAIR 20

Strange as it may seem, the Brown Tabby is among the rarer shorthairs. It may be that because some people do not realize how distinctive a cat a pedigree Brown Tabby is, with typical British broad round head, small ears and big round eyes, and black markings standing out from the sable background fur.

As with the Silver Tabby, the Brown Tabby appears in the other self colours, with the exception of White, Black and Red.

STANDARD

The basic standard and the scale of points is as described on page 80 for the British Shorthair.

Colour	Brilliant copper brown ground with dense black markings. Nose leather brick red. Pads black. Backs of legs from paw to heel black. For markings *see* pattern standards.
Eyes	Deep gold, copper or orange.
Faults	Brindling on uneven ground colour.
Withhold certificates	Incorrect eye colour. White anywhere.

TORTOISESHELL SHORTHAIR

The Tortoiseshell is a cat of great charm; its short coat of black, dark and light areas of red, evenly intermingled and distributed over the body, must show on the ears, face, feet and tail. A red blaze on the face is liked. There should be no white hairs. It is rare to find a perfectly marked cat with no brindling or tabby markings.

Tortoiseshell is in effect a female-only variety, as any males that are born are sterile. A self-coloured male of one of the colours in the coat is the best stud, but even this will be unlikely to produce more than one or two Tortoiseshell kittens in a litter. A Bi-colour could be tried, although this may introduce white into the coat (but then Tortoiseshell-and-whites are always popular). The best Torties are born dark and the colouring only becomes apparent as the cat grows.

STANDARD

The basic standard and scale of points is as described on page 80 for the British Shorthair.

Colour   A mixture of black, rich red and pale red evenly intermingled, with both colours clearly defined over the whole animal, but without any obvious patches of any colour, with the exception of a short narrow blaze on its face, which is permissible. Nose leather and pads pink, black or both.

Eyes   Brilliant copper or orange.

Faults   Tabby markings. Brindling. White anywhere. Colour unbroken on paws. Unequal balance of colour.

Chocolate Tortoiseshell (breed number 21b)—a mixture of chocolate and rich red, and Lilac Tortoiseshell (21c)—lilac and cream, are also now accepted.

TORTOISESHELL-AND-WHITE SHORTHAIR 22

The Tortoiseshell-and-whites are full of character, very affectionate and make excellent mothers. As with the Torties, the brilliant coloured patches of black, cream and red should stand out clearly, but with additional areas of white. Colour patches should cover the top of the head, ears, back and tail, and also part of the sides. A white blaze on the forehead is liked. The eyes should be copper or orange. Faults are blurring of the colours, tabby markings and brindling.

As this is another female-only variety, the best kind of stud is a Bi-colour (Black-and-white or Red-and-white) or a self-coloured cat of one of the colours in the coat, to try to produce kittens like the mother.

STANDARD

The basic standard and the scale of points is as described on page 80 for the British Shorthair.

Coat Colour   Patches of black, red and white. The patches of colour should be clear and well-defined, dense black, rich and pale red without any tabby markings. At least one third and not more than one half of the coat to be white, with patches of colour on the top of the head, ears, cheeks, back, tail, legs and flanks. A blaze is desirable.

Tortoiseshell-and-white shorthair

Eye colour   Deep orange or copper.

Nose leather and pads   Pink and/or black

Recently added to this variety are Blue, Chocolate, Lilac,
Tortoiseshell-and-white, and there is a further range of coat
colours under the Tortoiseshell Tabby classification, com-
prising Tortie Tabby, Tortie Silver Tabby, Tortie Spotted
and Tortie Silver Spotted; all comply to the standard
British Shorthair general type standard.

COLOURPOINTED BRITISH SHORTHAIR   40

These now comprise a complete family of recognized cats
that conform to the general type standard, although the scale
of points differs slightly from that for the patterned varieties
in that coat points are evenly split between texture/length
and colour/pattern. The full family includes selfs, tortie,
tabby and tortie tabby-pointed colours.

The tailless cat from the Isle of Man, or Rumpy as it is often called, is a cat on its own. Whilst it has very similar characteristics to the British shorthairs, the Manx must be quite definitely without a tail, that is, there should be a decided hollow without even a rudimentary tail. Cats without tails are also known in Japan and Malaya. Tradition has it that these cats first appeared on the Isle of Man after the wreck of a galleon from the Spanish Armada close to the coast.

It is quite difficult to breed true Manx: if two Manx cats are mated together they may produce some kittens with tails, some with stumps (known as Stumpie Manx) and some without tails. It seems that if Manx are bred exclusively over a succession of generations a 'lethal factor' may arise, causing the kittens to die before or shortly after birth.

Taillessness, depth of flank and high back legs help to give the characteristic 'rabbitty' gait, which is more of a hop than a walk. Roundness of the rump is essential for a good show specimen, with very high hindquarters and a short back. To find out if the cat is a true Manx, it should be possible to place the end of the thumb in the hollow at the end of the backbone, where the tail of another cat would begin. The vertebrae end at this point, whereas in other cats they continue down the tail. Although most cats make good use of their tails when jumping from a height, the Manx seems to jump just as well without one.

The Manx should have a 'double' coat, the top coat being soft and open and the undercoat thick, but many today seem to fail upon this point. All colours and markings are accepted. Although some bred in the United States have long coats, in Britain the Manx is essentially shortcoated. The large round head should have a slightly longer nose than that of the mainland British varieties, and the ears should have slightly pointed tips, not rounded. The Manx make very intelligent and amusing pets. They certainly have a very distinctive appearance.

STANDARD (with scale of points)

Head	Fairly round and large with prominent cheeks. Nose broad and straight, of medium length without break. Strong muzzle without any hint of snipiness. Firm chin and even bite.
Ears	Fairly tall, set rather high on the head and angled slightly outwards. Open at base tapering to a narrow, rounded tip. For head and ears 20 points
Eyes	Large and round. Colour preferably in keeping with coat colour. 5 points
Body	Solid, compact, with good breadth of chest and short back ending in a definite round rump. The rump to be higher than the shoulder. Flanks of great depth.
Legs	Of good substance with front legs short and well set to show good breadth of chest. Back legs longer than the front with powerful, deep thighs. For body, legs and paws 30 points

Coat	Double coated showing a well padded quality arising from a short, very thick undercoat and a slightly longer overcoat. The double quality of the coat is of far more importance than colour and markings, which should only be taken into account if all other points are equal. All colours and pattern are acceptable with the exception of the 'Siamese' pattern. 20 points
Taillessness	Absolute taillessness is essential. The rump should be felt to be completely rounded with no definite rise of bone or cartilage interfering with the roundness of the rump. 25 points

Faults
1. A rise of bone or cartilage at the end of the spine.
2. Lack of double coat.
3. Weak chin.

Withhold Challenge Certificate and 1st Place in kitten classes for:
1. Definite rise of bone or cartilage at the end of the spine interfering with the roundness of the ramp.
2. Uneven bite.
3. Any other anatomical abnormality (e.g. mobile or protruding xiphisternum, umbilical hernia, abnormal number of toes, etc.)

BLUE-CREAM SHORTHAIR   28

Another very attractive shorthaired variety, female only, with softly intermingled blue and cream. It is difficult to produce a Blue-cream without some patches. Faults are unbroken colour on the paws, and any white in the coat.

It is possible, by various matings, to breed several varieties using these cats, as described in connection with the longhaired Blue-creams on page 51.

STANDARD

The basic standard and the scale of points is as described

97

Blue-cream shorthair

on page 80 for the British Shorthair.

Coat colour   A mixture of medium blue and pale cream, evenly intermingled, with both colours clearly defined over the whole body, but without obvious patches of either colour, with the exception of a permissible, short blaze on the face.

Eye colour   Copper, orange or deep gold.

Nose leather and pads   Pink and/or blue.

Faults   Uneven balance of colour, colour unbroken on paws, brindling. Tabby markings and silver tipping permissible in kittens only.

Withhold Challenge Certificate and 1st Place in kitten classes for:

1. Unsound coats.
2. White anywhere.
3. Incorrect eye colour or rims or flecks of contrasting colour (in adults).
4. All other withholding faults as in the General Type Standard.

SPOTTED SHORTHAIR

First shown in the 1880s, the Spotties are a variety which for some reason vanished for a while and then reappeared as domestic pets in the 1950s. Judicious breeding has achieved the spotting in different coloured shorthairs, and they now frequently appear in litters with tabbies of the same background colour.

The type is typically British and usually good. The head should bear similar markings to those of the tabby, but otherwise there is no defined pattern for the markings. The spotting should be distinct from the background fur and as abundant as possible.

The most popular Spottie is the Silver, which has black spots, then the Brown, followed by the Red with deep red spotting. Apart from these any approved colouring is also permissible, as long as the spot colour is in keeping with the ground colour. The tail too should be spotted, but broken rings are allowed. The eye colour should be in keeping with the ground colour too. White or brindling in the coat are both faults.

Spotted Red shorthair

STANDARD

The basic standard and the scale of points is as described on page 80 for the British Shorthair.

The Spotted cat has the same head pattern as the Classic and Mackerel Tabbies. The pattern on the body and legs should consist of numerous, well-defined, oval, round or rosette-shaped spots which follow the Tabby pattern in distribution. The tail should have numerous, narrow rings or spots, the tip of the tail being the same colour as the markings.

Coat colour	Spotting to be of any colour accepted in the British Breeds with appropriate ground colour.
Eye colour	Silver cats with black spots – green or hazel. Brown cats with black spots – copper, orange or deep gold. All other colours – deep orange or copper.
Nose leather and pad	Corresponding to coat colour.
Faults	Incorrect, brindled or uneven ground colour.
Faults	Solid black, linked spots, bars.

BI-COLOUR SHORTHAIR 31

A recently recognized variety, as yet comparatively rare.
The history is similar to that of the Bi-colour longhairs and
these cats too are useful as studs in matings to Tortoiseshell-
and-whites. The colours which may be paired with white
are black, blue, chocolate, lilac, red and cream. The colour
division must be quite distinct, and there should be no white
hairs in the colour sections.

STANDARD

The basic standard and the sale of points is as described on
page 80 for the British Shorthair.

Colour
: Any accepted colour and white. The patches of
colour to be clear and evenly distributed.
Preferably one-third and not more than one-half
to be white. Face to be patched with colour.
White blaze and symmetry in design desirable.

Eyes
: Brilliant copper, orange or deep gold. Green
rims are a fault.

Faults
: Brindling. Tabby markings.

Withhold certificates
: For a predominance of white.

SMOKE BRITISH SHORTHAIR 36

From time to time, usually in litters of Blacks and Blues, kittens have been born that turned out to be Black or Blue Smokes. At first such kittens were registered as Any Other Variety, and had no standard of their own. As they were much admired when seen at the shows it was decided that they could be recognized and given open classes of their own.

STANDARD

The basic standard and the scale of points is as described on page 80 for the British Shorthair.

Coat colour	This is a genetically silver, non-tabby variety of British Shorthair. The top coat may be any recognized self or tortie colour(s). The undercoat to be silver, showing maximum contrast.
Eyes	Copper, orange or deep gold.
Paws	Paw pads and nose leather should correspond to coat colour; mingled with pink in Torties.

BRITISH TIPPED

A new variety of British shorthair has recently made its appearance, known as the British Tipped. The type is as for all British cats, with broad round head, small ears and short straight broad nose. The fur differs from all other British varieties in that the undercoat should be white, tipped with any recognized British self colour or they can be black, blue, chocolate or lilac tortie tipped. The Golden Tipped has a different breed number (75). The tipping must, of course, be the same colour on the back, flanks, head, ears and tail.

STANDARD

The basic standard and the scale of points is as described on page 80 for the British Shorthair.

Colour   The undercoat to be as white as possible. Coat on the back, flanks, head, ears and tail tipped with any recognized colour with the addition of brown, chocolate and lilac. Tipping should be evenly distributed to give a sparkling effect. The legs may be very slightly shaded with tipping, but the chin, stomach, chest and undertail should be as white as possible. Tabby markings or spots are faults (excepting ghost tail rings). Nose leather and pads appropriate to colour of coat tipping.

Eyes   Cats with black tipping – green. All other colours: copper, orange or deep gold.

Cream and Red Taby shorhair kittens

British Cream and Blue-cream shorthair kittens

FOREIGN SHORTHAIRED CATS

RUSSIAN BLUE

One of the foreign breeds with a soft short close-lying coat of seal-like appearance. It is thought that these cats came to Britain many years ago, brought from Russia on cargo ships trading between Archangel and this country. They were known as the Archangel cats or Blue Foreign type and it was not until the late 1940s that the present name was adopted. It must be appreciated that the Russian Blues seen today are the result of selective breeding, and that the name does not imply country of origin.

Russian Blues have slender lithe bodies, flat and narrow skulls, with receding foreheads, vivid green almond-shaped eyes and large pointed ears. The coat colours vary from medium to dark blue and must be the same all over. The fine bones and slender well-proportioned bodies make these cats look extremely distinguished.

The hind legs of this breed are longer than those of the British shorthairs. The dainty feet should be small and oval.

Russian Blue

These delightful elegant cats are becoming much favoured as pets, being of quiet disposition, but very affectionate. Their short silky fur is easy to groom, with hard hand stroking removing any dead hairs, and short daily brushing, keeping the coats looking immaculate.

STANDARD (with scale of points)

Colour	Clear blue and even throughout. In maturity free from tabby markings or shading. Medium blue is preferred.	15 points
Nose leather and pads	Blue	
Coat	Short, thick and very fine, standing up soft and silky like seal skin. Very different from any other breed. Coat is double so that it has a distinct silvery sheen. The texture and appearance of the coat is the breed's true criterion.	30 points
Body	Long and graceful in outline and carriage. Medium bone.	with legs and tail 20 points
Tail	Fairly long and tapering.	
Legs and feet	Long legs. Feet small and oval.	
Head	Short wedge with flat skull; forehead and nose straight forming an angle. Prominent whisker pads. Strong chin.	including ears 20 points
Eyes	Vivid green, wide apart, almond shape.	20 points
Ears	Large and pointed, wide at base and set vertically to the head. Skin of ears thin and transparent, with little inside hair.	
Faults	White or tabby markings. Cobby or heavy build. Square head. Yellow or blue in eyes. Siamese type is undesirable.	
Withhold certificates	White anywhere. Incorrect eye colour. Siamese type.	
Note	It is now possible to have a Russian White and a Russian Black, with similar standards.	

Usual Abyssinian

ABYSSINIAN

In 1868 a Mrs Barrett-Lennard brought a cat from Abyssinia to England and from the description given it appears to have been the forerunner of the breed known today. Experts agree that these African cats, although given the name 'Abyssinian' at that time, were not a breed as such. The Abyssinians we know today are the results of judicious breeding by British fanciers. They are very like those depicted in frescoes and statues in ancient Egypt.

The type is foreign, with a longish body and slender bones, but the coat is very distinctive. The fur should be a rich golden brown, ticked with black, the treble ticking to comprise three bands of colour on each hair in the 'usual' or original colour.

Abyssinians were recognized in Britain as long ago as 1882, and they were shown at the Crystal Palace show in about 1883. As well as 'Abyssinian' they were exhibited under various other names, such as Hare cat and Rabbit cat. As its fur was similar to that of the rabbit some considered that the Abyssinian was the result of cross-mating a cat and a rabbit, not realizing that this was impossible.

At the beginning of the century there was considerable argument about the choice of a name, and for a time the

Blue Abyssinian

breed was called the Bunny or British Ticked cat. Eventually the official name of Abyssinian was agreed.

As long ago as 1887 a kitten with a red coat appeared in a litter, but it is not known what happed to it. Afterwards it proved not to be too rare for red kittens to be born in litters of Usual Abyssinians (as the golden brown ones are called), but the red colour was not recognized and they had to be registered as Any Other Variety, not competing in the open Abyssianian classes. In 1957 the Reds, now Sorrel, were recognised. The standard differs only in the colour requirement; the lustrous copper fur, double or treble ticked with chocolate on a bright apricot base hair. Chin, lips and nostrils should be the colour of the base hair or cream. White here is undesirable, and white markings a bad fault. Bars on the legs, chest and tail, or a complete necklet, are undesirable. A kink in the tail is a fault. It is also possible to produce a Blue Abyssinian, which has blue grey fur ticked with deeper steel blue. The Blues have been registered since 1975. More recently registered colours and patterns are chocolate, lilac, fawn, red, cream, silvers and tortoiseshells of all the self colours except red and cream.

The Abyssinian has an amiable disposition, takes readily to a lead, is extremely intelligent and is in great demand as a pet and as a show cat. The cats are not prolific breeders, and four in a litter is about the average. Abyssinians from Britain have been exported all over the world and do well at foreign shows.

STANDARD (With scale of points)

Type	Foreign type of medium build, firm, lithe and muscular, never large or coarse. The head to be broad and tapering to a firm wedge set on an elegant neck. The body to be of medium length with fairly long tapering tail. A cobby cat is not permissible. For body 15 points
Head and ears	Head is a moderate wedge of medium proportions, the brow, cheeks and profile lines showing a gentle contour and the muzzle not sharply pointed. A shallow indentation forming the muzzle is desirable but a pinch is a fault. Ears set wide apart and pricked, broad at base, comparatively large, well cupped and preferably tufted. In profile the head shows a gentle rounding to the brow with a slight nose-break leading to a very firm chin. Head 15 points, ears 10 points
Eyes	Well apart, large, bright and expressive in an oriental setting. A squint is a fault. Colour, amber, hazel or green. 5 points
Tail	Broad at base, fairly long and tapering. Neither a whip nor a kink is permissible. 5 points
Legs and feet	Legs elegant, feet small and oval. 10 points
Coat	Short, fine and close lying with double, or preferably treble ticking, i.e. two or three bands of colour on each hair. For colour 20 points
Markings	It is required that the appropriate darker hair colour extends well up the back of the hind legs; also showing as a solid tip at the extreme end of the tail, and the absence of either is a fault. A line

of dark pigmentation is required around the eyes and absence of this is also a fault.

Undesirable markings are bars on the legs, chest and tail. An unbroken necklet is not permissible. The Abyssinian cat has a tendency to white in the immediate area of the lips and lower jaw and it is a fault if this white area extends on to the neck. A locket and other white markings are not permissible.   20 points

Colours

Usual 23 The body colour to be a rich golden brown, ticked with black and the base hair ruddy-orange or rich apricot. A pale or cold colour is a fault.

The belly and inside of legs to be a ruddy-orange or rich apricot to harmonize with the base hair on the rest of the body. Any spinal shading to be of deeper colour. The tip of the tail and the solid colour on the hind legs to be black. Nose leather to be brick red and pads to be black.

Sorrel 23a The body colour to be a lustrous copper red, ticked with chocolate and the base hair deep apricot. A pale or sandy colour is a fault.

The belly and inside of legs to be a deep-apricot to harmonize with the base hair on the rest of the body. Any spinal shading to be of deeper colour. The tip of the tail and the solid colour on the hind legs to be chocolate. Nose leather and pads to be pink.

Blue 23c The body colour to be blue-grey with a soft warm effect, ticked with deeper steel blue and the base hair pinkish mushroom.

The belly and inside of legs to be a pinkish mushroom to harmonize with the base hair on the rest of the body. Any spinal shading to be of deeper colour. The tip of the tail and the solid colour on the hind legs to be steel blue. Nose leather to be dark pink and pads to be mauvish-blue.

Any cat displaying a feature which is classed as not permissible (i.e. cobby type, whip tail; kink in tail; unbroken necklet; locket; other white markings, pinched muzzle or lack of muzzle indentation, pale or muddy eye colour, eyes not set in oriental setting or incorrect coat shading) shall not be awarded a first prize, a challenge certificate or a premier certificate.

There are a number of colour variations including Chocolate, Red, Cream and Torties in the new colourings.

BROWN BURMESE 27

In 1930 a female brown foreign-type cat was taken from Burma to North America. This cat was most attractive and much admired. As no brown male was available she was mated to a Siamese, and from the resultant litter and careful selective breeding the Burmese cat resulted. This became a recognized breed in the United States.

In 1949 a breeder imported from an American cattery the first pair seen in Britain. The queen came over already mated, but unfortunately the long period of quarantine told on her

Brown Burmese

Blue Burmese

health, and all the kittens died. In 1953 another male called Cas Gatos De Foong was imported from the United States. These two cats are the foundation of the breed in Britain. The first queen did not live long, but left progeny which have been of the highest value to fanciers. Since 1952 the Burmese have had breed numbers and their increased popularity may be judged by the number exhibited at shows today, and indeed in Britain they now have shows of their own.

In 1957 an outstanding brown male was imported from the USA, Champion Darsham Kudiram, and this proved a great asset in the breed as it brought new strains into the pedigree and helped to correct many faults. The Brown Burmese is the most popular colour.

Until 1955 Burmese were always thought of as brown cats, but in that year a female, mated back to her sire, Casa Gatos Darkee, produced the first Blue Burmese kitten, to be known as Sealcoat Blue Surprise. After the appearance of this cat the Blue Burmese quickly attained popularity. They were recognized in 1960.

The Blue played a large part in directing interest towards the possibility of producing other new colours, and additionally modifying these colours by blue dilution. From 1968

Chocolate Burmese

Reds and Creams were produced. The colour red was originally introduced from a shorthaired Ginger Tabby. By selective breeding over many years plain coats were achieved, and the original barring has largely disappeared. Cream is the blue-diluted form of the Red. The variety was recognized in 1971.

The Chocolate and Lilac varieties arose as a result of the import of cats into Britain in 1969–70. These cats were either Chocolate or Brown carrying chocolate. When the chocolate gene was introduced into the British Burmese the cats were very American in appearance, being stocky, short in the leg and tail, and rounder in the head than the British varieties. Selective breeding has subsequently improved the type considerably. It is difficult however to produce a cat of the correct 'warm milk chocolate' with no dark mask. In order to avoid contrast between the mask and body colours the show cats are often darker than is strictly correct.

Lilac Burmese have become very popular. As young kittens they are difficult to distinguish from Chocolates, and sometimes impossible until they are eight to ten weeks old. As with the Chocolates there is a wide range of colour, from a bluish lilac to a creamy fawn. Type is usually very good.

Lilac Burmese

When sex-linked Red and Cream Burmese are mated to Brown, Blue, Chocolate and Lilac Burmese, Tortoiseshell females are produced. Chocolate and Lilac Torties are only produced when the appropriate gene for dilution is carried by both parents, and these two varieties were first registered in 1973. The Brown and Blue Torties were, in contrast, produced as early as 1964, when the Red and Cream programmes were at their beginnings. The Torties are bred principally for type, and in consequence receive more points for type and less for colour.

It has now become possible to produce Burmese in ten colours: for instance if a Red male, brown based, carrying blue and chocolate, mates a Brown Tortie, also carrying blue and chocolate, the kittens could be of six different plain colours or of the four different Tortie colours.

Since 1977 when the four Tortie colours were finally accepted, all the Burmese colours have championship status. More important is the fact that while blue has diluted the normal colour or red or chocolate has replaced the brown, the cat is still as much a Burmese as the original Brown Burmese and the type and basic character of the cat remains unchanged.

Red Burmese

STANDARD (with scale of points)

The Burmese is an elegant cat of a foreign type, which is positive and quite individual to the breed. Any suggestion of either Siamese type, or the cobbiness of a British cat, must be regarded as a fault. Temperament is awarded 5 points.

Body, legs and tail The body should be of medium length and size, feeling hard and muscular, and heavier than its appearance indicates. The chest should be strong and rounded in profile, the back straight from shoulder to rump. Legs should be slender and in proportion to the body: hind legs slightly longer than front: paws neat and oval in shape. The tail should be straight and of medium length, not heavy at base, and tapering only slightly to a rounded tip without bone defect. A visible kink or other bone defect in the tail is a fault, precluding the award of a challenge certificate. Points are awarded as follows; body 20 points, legs and paws 5 points, tail 5 points.

Cream Burmese kittens

Head, ears and eyeset The head should be slightly rounded on top, with good breadth between the ears, having wide cheek bones and tapering to a short blunt wedge. The jaw should be wide at the hinge and the chin firm. A muzzle pinch is a bad fault. Ears should be medium in size, set well apart on the skull, broad at the base with slightly rounded tips, the outer line of the ears, continuing the shape of the upper part of the face. This may not be possible in mature males, who develop a fullness of cheek. In profile the ears should be seen to have a slight forward tilt. There should be a distinct nose break, and in profile the chin should show a strong lower jaw. The eyes, which must be set well apart, should be large and lustrous, the top line of the eye showing a straight oriental slant towards the nose, the lower line being rounded. Either round or oriental eyes are a fault. Head 20, ears 10, eyeset 5 points

Eye colour Eyes should be any shade of yellow from chartreuse to amber, with golden yellow pre-

Tortoiseshell Burmese

ferred. Green eyes are a serious fault in Brown Burmese, but Blue Burmese may show a slight fading of colour. Green eyes with more blue than yellow pigmentation must preclude the award of a challenge certificate.   5 points

Coat The coat should be short, fine and satin-like in texture, lying close to the body. The glossy coat is a distinctive feature of the Burmese.

Coat condition 10, colour 10, textures 5 points

Condition Cats should be well muscled, with good weight for size; lively and alert.

Colours

General considerations In all colours, the underparts will be lighter than the back. In kittens and adolescents, allowances should be made for faint Tabby barring and overall, a lighter colour than adults. The presence of a few white hairs may be overlooked in an otherwise excellent cat, but a noticeable number of white hairs, or a white patch is a serious fault, precluding the award of a Challenge Certificate.

Brown 27   In maturity the adult should be a rich warm Seal brown, shading almost imperceptibly to a slightly lighter shade on the underparts; apart from this and slightly darker ears and mask, there should be no shading or marking of any kind. Very dark colour, bordering on black, is incorrect. Nose leather rich brown, foot pads brown.

Blue 27a   In maturity the adult should be a soft silver grey only very slightly darker on the back and tail. There should be a distinct silver sheen on rounded areas such as ears, face and feet. Nose leather very dark grey, foot pads pinkish grey.

Chocolate 27b   In maturity the overall colour should be a warm milk chocolate. Ears and mask may be slightly darker, but legs, tail and lower jaw should be the same colour as the back. Evenness of colour overall very desirable. Nose leather warm chocolate brown, foot pads a brick pink shading to chocolate.

Lilac 27c   In maturity the coat colour should be a pale, delicate dove-grey, with a slightly pinkish cast giving a rather faded effect. Ears and mask may be slightly deeper in colour. Nose leather lavender pink, foot pads shell pink in kittens, becoming lavender pink in adults.

Red 27d   In maturity the coat colour should be light tangerine. Slight Tabby markings may be found on the face, and small indeterminate markings elsewhere (except on sides and belly) are permissible in an otherwise excellent cat. Ears should be distinctly darker than the back. Nose leather and foot pads pink.

Brown Tortie 27e *(Normal Tortie)*

The coat should be a mixture of brown and red without any obvious barring. The colour and markings are not so important as the Burmese type, which should be excellent. Nose leather and foot pads plain or blotched, brown and pink.

Cream 27f   In maturity the coat colour should be rich cream. Slight Tabby markings may be found on the face, and small indeterminate markings elsewhere (except on the sides and belly) are permissible in an otherwise excellent cat. Ears should be only slightly darker than the back coat colour. Nose leather and foot pads pink.

Blue Tortie 27g *(Blue Cream)*

The coat should be a mixture of blue and cream without any obvious barring. Colour and markings are not so important as the Burmese type, which should be excellent. Nose leather and foot pads plain or blotched, blue and pink.

Chocolate Tortie 27h   The coat should be a mixture of chocolate and red without any obvious barring. The colour and markings are not so important as the Burmese type, which should be excellent. Nose leather and foot pads plain or blotched, chocolate and pink.

Lilac Tortie 27j *(Lilac Cream)*   The coat should be lilac with shades of cream. Nose leather and paw pads plain or blotched lilac and pink.

TONKINESE   74

The result of crossing Siamese with Burmese and first recognized in North America. The coat colour is determined by the point colour of the Siamese used. Tonkinese are only bred to Tonkinese and not back to their parents.

The overall impression is that of a well-proportioned and well-muscled cat, of medium foreign type. Head a moderate wedge, neither pointed nor square-muzzled. Ears slightly taller than wide, pricked forward. Eyes more open than oriental but not round. Body medium to long, with slim legs and neat oval feet.

ORIENTAL ANDREX-COATED SHORTHAIRS
HAVANA 29

The Havana is a man-made breed which owes its existence to a small group of breeders who commenced work towards its production in the early 1950s. It was the first shorthair breed of Siamese body type, but without the Siamese coat pattern, to be recognized by the Governing Council of the Cat Fancy. It gained championship status in 1958, and was then known as the Chestnut Brown Foreign. In 1970 this name was officially amended to Havana, which was the original breed name chosen by the founder breeders. It is now very popular and classes at the shows are well filled.

The body type of the Havana is similar to that of the Siamese but its coat is a rich warm brown, and is quite different in appearance from the brown coat of the Burmese. The eyes should be a distinct green.

The kittens, which are always in great demand both as pets and as show cats, are born the colour they will remain when fully adult. They should show no shading to a darker or lighter colour on any part of their body, except perhaps during the summer moult when the old coat sometimes appears rusty. The nose, lips and whiskers are brown like the fur, but the pads are of a pinkish shade, and very distinctive.

ORIENTAL SHORTHAIRED STANDARD (with scale of points)

General
: The Oriental should be a beautifully balanced animal with head and ears carried on a slender neck and with a long svelte body supported on fine legs and feet with a slender, whipped tail free from abnormalities. The head and profile should be wedge shaped, neither round nor pointed. The body, legs, feet, head and tail should all be in proportion giving a well balanced appearance. The expression should be alert and intelligent. The cat should be in excellent physical condition.

Head, neck and ears
: Head, long and well proportioned with width between the ears and narrowing in perfectly straight lines to a fine muzzle, forming a triangle with no break at the whiskers or pinch. In profile the nose should be straight, free from any stop or dip and the chin should be strong with a level bite. The tip of the chin should line up with the tip of the nose in the same vertical plane. The neck should be long and slender. The ears should be large, pricked and wide at the base with their setting continuing the lines of the wedge.   Head and neck 15 points, ears 5 points

Eye shape
: Oriental in shape and slanting towards the nose with good width between.   5 points

Body, legs and paws
: Medium in size. Long and svelte with a tight abdomen. Legs long and slim. Hind legs higher than the front legs. The body and legs to be firm and well muscled throughout. Paws small and oval.   Body 15, legs and paws 5 points

Tail	Long and tapering. Not blunt ended and free from any bone structure abnormality. 5 points
Coat	Very short and fine in texture. Glossy and close lying. Even and sound throughout in adults and free from any flakes of dead skin. 5 points
Eye colour	Always green without flecks of different colour. Clear vivid green for Havanas. 15 points (except tabby patterns, 10 points)
Coat colour	For the Havana, rich warm chestnut brown, not dark or toned. 30 points (except tabby patterns, 35 points)
Nose leather	Brown or pinkish brown.
Paw pads	Solid brown or solid pinkish brown.

Disqualify exhibits for:
1. Visible kink.
2. White locket, white buttons, white belly spot or white toe(s).

Foreign Lilac

ORIENTAL LILAC 29c

The Oriental Lilac was developed from the Havana and was recognized for championship status in 1977. It has a most attractive coat of a subtle pink-toned frosty grey, with pinkish nose leather and pads. The eyes should be a definite green. Its unusual colouring combined with the Siamese body type make it one of the up-and-coming shorthaired breeds. At present there are few Foreign Lilac cats at stud, so some breeders are mating the Foreign Lilac to Havanas. Once like-to-like matings are more usual practice the numbers of Foreign Lilacs bred will most certainly increase dramatically.

STANDARD

The basic standard and the scale of points is as described on page 121 for the Oriental Shorthair.

Colour   Frosty grey with a distinct pinkish tone. Nose leather and pads pinkish. Colour too blue or too fawn is a fault. Other faults as for the Havana.

FOREIGN WHITE 35

White cats with foreign type have always been known to appear occasionally in litters, and when they did so they have been very much admired. The prospect of creating a regular breed of these cats was opened up in the early 1960s when a small group of fanciers began a careful programme of breeding. The resulting variety has the body outline and type of the Siamese as well as the brilliant blue eye colour of Siamese; the coat is short, fine and glossy, and it is pure white.

The most popular breeding system is to mate the Foreign White to Seal-point Siamese, as this is the most likely combination to produce the deep blue eye colour. In the resulting litters some of the kittens will be Siamese and some Foreign White. In fact the Foreign White is strictly speaking a Siamese cat, in which all colour points and the beige body colour have been masked by the pure white coat.

The breed was granted full championship status in 1977 and kittens are now in great demand, making beautiful show cats and intelligent pets.

STANDARD (with scale of points)

Coat	Pure white, short and close-lying. Texture 10 points, colour 15 points
Head and ears	Long and well-proportioned, narrowing in straight lines to a fine muzzle with straight profile. Nose leather pink, ears large and pricked with width between. 20 points
Eyes	Almond shaped and slanting, clear, brilliant blue. Eye shape 5 points, colour 15 points
Body	Long and slender, the rump carried higher than the shoulders. Well muscled and elegant. 15 points
Legs	Long and proportionately slender, paws neat and oval. Pads pink. 10 points
Tail	Long and tapering, whip-like, no kink. 10 points
Certificates shall be withheld	For coloured hairs and black discolouration on nose leather or paw pads in Adult Foreign White Cats.

Foreign White

ORIENTAL BLACK 37

A new and most attractive example of the foreign varieties, developed from crosses between Havana and Seal-point Siamese. The short fine close-lying jet black fur should be without white hairs or rusty tinge. The type is Siamese, with long head and large ears. The eyes of oriental shape, should be green. Faults are squinting, kinked tail, white hairs and any white marking in the fur. Granted championship status 1980.

STANDARD

The basic standard and the scale of points is as described on page 121 for the Oriental Shorthair.

Type   As Siamese.

Eyes   Oriental in shape, colour green.

Colour   Jet black to the roots. No rusty tinge or white hairs, although the presence of both these features in otherwise good kittens is acceptable. Nose leather black, pads black or brown.

CORNISH REX

Although many new breeds have appeared in recent years, all but two have been produced by selective breeding. The two exceptions to this are the Cornish and Devon Rex; the word Rex refers to the coats, which wave or curl due to a natural mutation affecting the hair structure.

The first Rex cat appeared in 1950 in a litter of farm kittens bred by Mrs Ennismore of Bodmin Moor, Cornwall. She was puzzled by the wavy-coated red and white kittens with curly whiskers and decided to consult her veterinary surgeon, who remembered that Rex rabbits had evolved in the same way. She advised that the kitten, named Kallibunker, be mated to his mother. This was done and, of the resulting kittens, two more were wavy-coated, although the mother was a normal straight-coated female. Experimental breeding then commenced under the supervision of Brian Stirling-Webb, who advised outcrossing to pedigree shorthair breeds. The resultant progeny, which were straight-coated, were mated back to the parents, when the proportion of Rex-coated to straight-coated kittens appeared in a 1:1 ratio, thus proving the Rex gene to be truly recessive.

The coat of these cats, named Cornish Rex after their county of origin in Britain, is very soft and dense and is completely lacking in guard hairs. Any colour, including the Siamese pattern, can be bred depending on the outcrosses used. The first Cornish Rex having been bred from farm stock of mongrels had more British type, but by using outcrosses only of foreign type, breeders managed to produce fine-boned and elegant creatures, resembling the ancient Egyptian cats in outline. They have short, dense, fine coats, forming waves over the body, and long, fine, whiplike tails.

Si-Rex is the name given to a Rex cat showing Siamese colour restrictions. It is not a variety.

Because of their intelligent and affectionate personalities, Cornish Rex are much in demand. Rex mutants have also appeared since 1950 in East Germany and North America. They also have medium to long heads with flat skulls and straight profiles; large ears set high on the head; almond shaped medium sized eyes, the colour in keeping with the coat colouring; and long slender bodies.

STANDARD (with scale of points)

Coat	Short and plushy without guard hairs, should curl, wave or ripple particularly on back and tail. Whiskers and eyebrows crinkled and of good length. All coat colours acceptable but any white markings must be symmetrical, except in Tortoiseshell-and-white. 35 points
Head	Medium wedge. Head length about one-third greater than the maximum width, narrowing to a strong chin. The skull to be flat. In profile a straight line to be seen from centre of forehead to end of nose. Ears large, set rather high on the head, wide at base, tapering to rounded tips. Head 15 points, whiskers and eyebrows 5 points
Eyes	Oval shaped, medium in size, colour in keeping with coat colour. 10 points
Ears	Large, set rather high on head, wide at base, tapering to rounded tips and well-covered with fine fur. 10 points

Body and legs	Body hard and muscular, slender and of medium length. Legs long and straight, giving an appearance of being high on the legs. Paws small, oval.
	20 points
Tail	Long, fine and tapering. 5 points

DEVON REX   33a

In 1950 Miss Beryl Cox, living in Buckfastleigh, found a curly-coated male kitten near a tin mine on the Devon Moors. Having read of the Cornish Rex, she assumed this kitten, which she named Kirlee, to be a close relative. She contacted Brian Stirling-Webb, the breeder, who took Kirlee, with the intention of breeding him to the Cornish females which were still kittens. Strange as it seemed at the time, all the resultant litters had straight coats. Many matings were tried without achieving Rex kittens; geneticists then concluded that the Cornish and Devon Rex were genetically incompatible, and responsible breeders do not cross-breed the two varieties.

Although Kirlee was somewhat similar in appearance to the Cornish Rex, his head was very different, being wide-

White Devon Rex

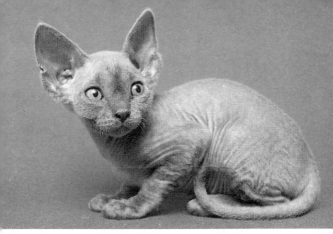

Blue Devon Rex kitten

cheeked, with huge low-set ears, giving him a 'pixie' look. Because of this unique appearance the outcrosses had to be chosen with great care; Burmese have been used with some success.

The Devon Rex have the intelligence and affection of the Cornish, but they also have a wicked sense of humour to match their elfin looks, and will do anything to attract attention.

The coat of the Devon feels coarser than that of the Cornish and, when examined under a microscope, proves to have some guard hairs, which tend to be brittle. The whiskers are curly but appear short, as they tend to break off. Kirlee's colour was mole grey, but now as a result of systematic breeding the Devons appear in all colours as well as the various Siamese patterns. White is acceptable only in the Tortie-and-white.

The German and North American mutations have been test-mated with the Devon Rex, but no other Rex variety has proved compatible.

Both the Cornish and the Devon Rex were officially recognized in 1967 and since then many have become champions.

Black Smoke Devon Rex

STANDARD (with scale of points)

Coat
: Very short and fine, wavy and soft. Whiskers and eyebrows crinkled, rather coarse and of medium length. All coat colours acceptable. Any white markings to be a disqualifying fault in Siamese pattern Devon Rex.　　40 points

Head
: Wedge-shaped with full cheeks. Short muzzle with strong chin and whisker break. Nose with a strongly marked stop. Forehead curving back to flat skull. Ears large, set rather low, wide at base, tapering to rounded tops and well covered with fine fur.　　Head 20 points, ears 10 points

Eyes
: Wide set, large oval shaped and sloping towards outer edges of ears. Colour in keeping with coat colour or (but not in Si-Rex) chartreuse-green or yellow.　　5 points

Body, legs and neck
: Body hard and muscular, slender and of medium length, broad in chest, carried high on slim legs, with length of hind legs emphasized. Paws small and oval, neck slender.　　20 points

Tortoiseshell Devon Rex

Tail	Long, fine and tapering, well covered with short fur.

5 points

KORAT 34

Some years ago these attractive cats were imported into the United States from Thailand but were not seen in Britain until comparatively recently. They are now recognized, with championship status, and the numbers are increasing. They have foreign type, small heads, heart-shaped faces and large ears. The eyes should be a brilliant green, but an amberish tinge is not considered a fault. Their unusual coats are silver-blue in colour, giving the fur a distinctive sheen.

STANDARD (with scale of points)

Head and ears — When viewed from the front the head is heart-shaped, with breadth between and across the eyes, gently curving to a well-developed but neither shapely pointed nor squared muzzle. Forehead large, flat.   Profile 6, width 5 points
    Ears large and with a rounded tip and large

Korat

	flare at base, set high on head, giving an alert expression. Ear set 5 points
Eyes	Large and luminous, brilliant green but amber acceptable. Shape and placement 15 points, breadth between 4 points, eye colour 5 points
Body	Medium-sized and semi-cobby. 15 points
Legs and paws	In proportion to body, paws oval. 5 points
Tail	Medium length, tapering to rounded tip. 5 points
Coat	Single, hair short to medium, glossy and fine and lying close to the body. Length 4 points, texture 4 points, close-lying 2 points
Condition	Perfect physical condition, muscular, physically alert appearance. 5 points
Colour	Any shade of blue all over tipped with silver, the more silver the better. Without shading or tabby markings. Nose leather and lips, dark blue or lavender. Paw pads dark blue ranging to lavender with pinkish tinge. 20 points

ORIENTAL TABBY   38, 41, 44, 45

For some years, cats with body outline similar to the Siamese, but with very different body colourings and coat patterns have been produced by careful selective breeding.

Some have the typical spotting of the British shorthairs, others have classic tabby markings, and there are also Tortoiseshells, Smokes and Shadeds. Referred to in general as the Orientals, they come under various headings. Oriental Tortoiseshell in seven colours; Oriental Shaded in any of the accepted Oriental Shorthair colours, likewise Oriental Smokes, but the Oriental Tabby can be in either spotted, classic, mackerel or tipped pattern, and there are now 32 recognized colours, which make a total of 128 possible Oriental Tabbies, ranging from Brown Spotted (breed number 38) to Fawn Tortie Silver Ticked (breed number 45ys), covering championship to preliminary status.

GENERAL STANDARD

The basic standard and the scale of points is as described on page 121 for the Oriental Shorthair.

The Oriental Tabby should be a beautifully balanced animal with head and ears carried on a slender neck with a long svelte body supported on fine legs and feet with a slender, whipped tail free from abnormalities. The head and profile should be wedge-shaped, neither round nor pointed. The body, legs, feet, head and tail should all be in proportion giving a well balanced appearance. The expression should be alert and intelligent. The cat should be in excellent physical condition. The Oriental Tabby has a tendency to white in the immediate area of the lips and lower jaw. It is a serious fault if this extends to the throat and/or muzzle. In Blue, Lilac and Cream Oriental Tabbies, the colour contrast between the spotting and the ground colour is less than that required in Brown, Chocolate and Red Tabbies.

Head, neck and ears   Head long and well proportioned with width between the ears and narrowing in perfectly straight lines to a fine muzzle and forming a triangle with no break at the whiskers

Oriental Spotted Tabby

or pinch. In profile the nose should be straight, free from any stop or dip and the chin should be strong with a level bite. The tip of the chin should line up with the tip of the nose in the same vertical plane. The neck should be long and slender. The ears should be large, pricked and wide at the base with their setting continuing the lines of the wedge.

Eye shape and setting Oriental in shape and slanting towards the nose with good width between.

Body, legs and paws Medium in size, long and svelte with a tight abdomen. Legs long and slim. Hind legs higher than the front legs. The body and legs to be firm and well muscled throughout. Paws small and oval.

Tail Long and tapering. Not blunt ended and free from any abnormality of the bone structure.

Coat Glossy, very short and fine in texture.

The Oriental Smoke is a developing breed fast catching the attention of breeders and the general public. It has the body type of the Siamese and is bred in a wide range of colours: any colour that appears in Oriental Shorthairs is accepted, with a near-white undercoat, which should be in the proportion of approximately one-third to two-thirds of the total hair length in adults. The degree of contrast on the head and face should match the body as closely as possible, with too much silver giving the appearance of clear tabby markings being undesirable. Some faint ghost tabby markings may be evident on the body, especially in kittens, but distinct tabby markings in adults are definitely undesirable.

STANDARD

The basic standard and the scale of points is as described on page 121 for the Oriental Shorthair.

Eyes Green with no flecks of contrasting colour. In Red and Cream Smokes the eye colour may be less intense.

Nose leather, eye rims and paw pads Always in accordance with the basic colour.

SCALE OF POINTS

This is in accordance with the Oriental Selfs other than Tabbies, with 50 points being awarded for type and 50 points for colour and coat.

Certificates or first prizes in Kitten Open Classes are withheld for scattered white hairs and for other general Oriental withholding points, which are: weak chink and/or even bite, any abnormality of the bone structure of the tail, incorrect eye colour, or any fleck of a different colour in the eye. Coat long, open or coarse in texture or any other fault applicable to all breeds.

The Oriental/Foreign Shorthair varieties with their close-lying, fine-textured, flossy coats have proliferated in recent years from the original self-coloured Siamese type and the popularity of these agile, playful and soft-voiced cats still continues to increase.

Oriental Smoke

ASIAN GROUP

This group comprises cats of Burmese type, but of non-Burmese coat colour, pattern or length. The Asian cats are to the Burmese as Orientals are to the Siamese.

ASIAN SELF   72

The Self variety of the Asian cat includes the Bombay, which is effectively the Black of the group, with a close-lying coat that looks like shimmering black patent leather. Apart from eight self colours, here are also five Asian Torties.

BURMILLA   72 43 Shaded

This is an agouti cat, the Shaded variety of the Asian group. The coat in both the Standard and the Silver varieties may be shaded or tipped. The colours are as for the Asian Selfs. In Silvers, the colours may be reduced in intensity. The undercoat should be as pale as possible in Standard varieties and nearly white in Silver varieties.

Foreign Red

ASIAN SMOKE 72 42

The Smoke variety is a non-agouti. Coat colour may be as
for Asian Selfs, with a silvery white or near-white undercoat,
which should be between one-third and half the total hair
length in adults with ghost tabby markings.

ASIAN TABBIES

This breed covers all the tabby coat patterns: Spotted (72
38); Classic (72 41); Mackerel (72 44) and Ticked (72 45).

GENERAL ASIAN TYPE

Head	Short wedge with a distinct nose break.
Ears	Medium to large in size with rounded tips.
Eyes	Depending on variety; any colour but gold preferred in Self.
Body	Medium length with firm muzzle.
Legs and paws	Of medium length, paws tending towards oval.
Tail	Medium to long and carried proudly.
Coat	Fine and close-lying to the body.

SIAMESE CATS

Of all the pedigree cats in Britain today the Siamese is one of the most popular breeds, and the numbers registered are steadily on the increase. The origin of the breed cannot be traced, although the head and body lines are like those of the cats once worshipped in Egypt. Apparently the first known pair of these exotic cats was brought to England in 1884 by Mr Gould, the Consul General in Bangkok, from the Royal Palace there. Similar cats had been guarded and treasured in the Royal palaces and temples for many years, and were considered of such value that few were ever given away, and then only as presents to one or two very honoured people.

With their lovely body lines, colouring, high intelligence and air of mystery it is easy to believe that the Siamese we know today are descendants of the Royal Cats of Siam. A Mrs Vyvyan and Miss Forestier Walker were among the first to own Siamese in England, and it is from their famous Tiam-o-Shan that many of the present-day cats are descended.

The Siamese is of medium size with a thin svelte body, fine boned and with long slim legs. The back legs are higher than the front, terminating in the distinctive oval or spoon-shaped feet. The head is long with good width between the ears, narrowing in straight lines to a fine muzzle and firm chin. There should be no pinch and the overall shape should be a wedge head carried on a long neck. The ears should be large, pricked and wide at the base. The eyes are a brilliant blue and oriental in shape. The tail is long, whiplike and tapering, with no kink. The coat is short, glossy and close lying.

Siamese love companionship and fret if they are left alone; they become very attached to their owners. If a cat has to be confined outside the house it is kinder to provide it with another cat as a companion. Siamese more than any other breed enjoy the company of people, and seem to understand all that is said to them.

They should not be overfed. Many Siamese cannot take milk, but others show no ill effects if given sparing quantities. The kittens particularly seem less able to take milk than the kittens of other varieties, and if it causes diarrhoea one should simply stop giving it. Fresh water should be put down daily for drinking.

Siamese love plenty of toys with which to play, and make lively, alert and highly intelligent pets. They take readily to the lead, and may sometimes be seen accompanying their owners on walks in parks and open spaces.

They are naturally prolific breeders, coming into season at an early age and producing litters of five or six kittens as a rule. They are quite persistent in making their wants known and have a distinctive and rather loud cry which is quite different from that of, for example, the Persian cat. The cry of a calling Siamese queen can be quite raucous.

The kittens are white when born, and the points do not begin to show until after the first week or so. The true point colouring may not show until the cat is about a year old.

There are now many recognized varieties of Siamese (the Siamese Cat Club has been at work improving the breed since 1901), starting with the original and still most popular Seal-point. Following the Seal-point in popularity are the Blue-point, the Chocolate-point and the Lilac-point. The newest varieties are the Tabby-point, Red-point, Tortie-point and Cream-point.

GENERAL STANDARD

The Siamese Cat should be a beautifully balanced animal with head, ears and neck carried on a long svelte body, supported on fine legs and feet with a tail in proportion. The head and profile should be wedge-shaped, neither round nor pointed. The mask complete, connected by tracings with the ears (except in kittens), the eyes a clear brilliant blue. Expression alert and intelligent.

Type:

Body and tail   Medium in size, body long and svelte, legs proportionately slim, hind legs slightly higher than front legs, feet small and oval, tail long and tapering and free from any kink. The body, legs and feet should all be in proportion giving the whole a well balanced appearance.

Head and ears	Head long and well proportioned carried upon an elegant neck, with width between the ears narrowing in perfectly straight lines to a fine muzzle, with straight profile, strong chin and level bite. Ears rather large and pricked, wide at base.
Eyes	Oriental in shape and slanting towards the nose, but with width between.
Points	Mask, ears, feet and tail dense and clearly defined colour, matching in basic colour on all points, showing clear contrast between points and body colour. Mask complete and (except in kittens) connected by tracings with the ears.
Coat	Very short and fine in texture, glossy and close-lying. Colours as per individual colour standards, any shading to appear on back and sides. Bib, chest and belly to be pale.
Notes:	Definition of Squint: a cat is said to have a squint when the eyes are so placed that they appear to look permanently at the nose.
	White toes or toe automatically disqualify an exhibit. It is important to note that the standard with regard to type is the same for all Siamese cats.

SIAMESE: SEAL-POINT   24

The original variety, the Seal-point Siamese is also the most poplar. The body colour is cream, shading gradually into pale warm fawn on the back. Kittens are paler in colour. The mask, ears, legs, feet and tail are a dense and clearly defined seal brown with no trace of brindling. The mask is complete and (except in kittens) connected by tracing with the ears.

SCALE OF POINTS

The following scale is applicable to all Siamese.

	Type	Colour and Coat
Head	15	
Ears	5	
Eyes	5	15
Body	15	
Legs and feet	5	
Tail	5	10
Points		15
Body		10
Coat texture		
Total	**50**	**50**

SIAMESE: BLUE-POINT 24a

Blue points are very popular and most attractive with glacial
white body colouring and blue points. Unfortunately the
colour is not always the desired glacial white shading to blue
on the flanks. Some tend to be too fawn in body colour and
too slate coloured and dark in the points, a fault which should
be bred out by selective breeding from cats of the correct
colour. The eyes, as in Seal-points must be oriental in shape
and in colour a clear vivid blue. The blue points should all be
of matching colour and the ears not a darker shade as
sometimes happens. A close coat of finest texture is required.
Nose leather and paw pads should be blue.

SIAMESE: CHOCOLATE-POINT 61b

Although Chocolate-points have occurred in Seal-point litters from the earlier days of Siamese, they were not officially recognized as a separate variety until 1950.

The body colour is ivory and the points milk chocolate. Body shading if present must be to the colour of the points. Great emphasis should be laid on the term 'milk' chocolate as opposed to 'plain' chocolate in the points colour. Unfortunately there seem to be far more cats of the darker shade than the desired lighter hue. These darker-pointed Chocolates tend to develop heavy body shading as they mature and do not retain the correct ivory colour.

SIAMESE: LILAC-POINT 24c

Lilac-points were originally bred in the USA where they were known as Frost-points. The first born in England were in a litter of Blue-points from two Blue-point parents, both of which carried the necessary chocolate factor to produce these colour points.

Lilac-points have magnolia-coloured bodies which seldom darken with age and the points are pinkish grey. The nose leather is the colour of faded lilac and the eyes a vivid blue. The desired points colour is not easy to attain and many lilacs are far too blue. They can appear in any Siamese litter where both parents carry both Blue and Chocolate genes. When bred Lilac to Lilac they always breed true to colour.

SIAMESE: TABBY-POINT 32

Known for a number of years as the Shadow- or Lynx-point,
this attractive variety was granted recognition in 1966 under
the name of Tabby-point. It differs from the solid colour
Siamese in that striped markings replace the solid points. It
should have a pale body colour free from markings. The ears
should be solid with no stripes but with a distinct thumb
mark. The mask must have clearly defined stripes and the
whisker pad should be spotted. The legs have broken stripes
with solid markings on the back of the hind legs. The tail
must have clearly defined rings and a solid tip. The nose
leather may either conform to the recognized standard for its
particular colour or be pink. All colours are acceptable in the
Tabby-points: seal, blue, chocolate, lilac, red, cream,
cinnamon, caramel or fawn.

SIAMESE: RED-POINT 32a

The Red-points were first recognized in Britain in 1966 after many years of dedicated breeding by Dr Nora Archer and Ann Ray. They are very handsome cats, with warm white body colour with shading, if any, to tone with the points. The mask, ears and tail are bright reddish gold. The legs and feet will be paler in colour but the bright colour should show at the rear of the hind legs below the hocks. Barring and striping on mask, legs and tail is permissible. Freckles may occur on nose, paw pads, lips, eyelids and ears. Nose leather, eye rims and paw pads pink; eyes a brilliant intense blue, the deeper the better.

SIAMESE: TORTIE-POINT 32b (1–4, 7–9)

A Tortie-point is invariably female and is a member of the
Red-point family. Much of their charm lies in the very varied
appearance of their points. It has been said that no two
Torties are ever exactly alike in their distribution of point
colours. The basic point colours are seal, blue, chocolate, lilac,
cinnamon, caramel and fawn, and red or cream markings in
the points are essential. The body colour should be as in
equivalent solid colour Siamese.

Unfortunately some Seal Torties show very heavy body
shading, which is undesirable and should be bred out. The
type and characteristics should be as for other Siamese.

Resembling Tabby-points and complementing the full
range of Tabby-point colours, these cats have patches of red,
cream or both irregularly distributed over the tabby pattern
on the points.

SIAMESE: CREAM-POINT 32c

Cream-points are a later variety of Siamese to be granted recognition. Their pastel colouring is delicate and distinctive. They have been produced by selective breeding from Red-points carrying the blue factor. The body colour is creamy white, shading, if any, to tone with the points. Mask, ears and tail cool-toned cream with a powdery look. The legs and feet will be slightly paler in colour but definite colour should show at the rear of the hind legs below the hock. The nose leather, eye rims and paw pads are pink, eyes a brilliant intense blue.

Barring or striping on the points is not considered a serious fault, and nor is slight freckling in a mature cat.

More recently Cinnamon-points, Caramel-points and Fawn-points have gained recognition, with points colours respectively as follows: warm cinnamon brown on ivory body colour; brownish grey on off-white (magnolia) body and warm pale rosy mushroom on off-white (magnolia) body.

PET CATS

Of the many millions of domestic cats in the world, the majority are non-pedigree or mongrel cats, and these are generally referred to simply as pet cats. Both pedigree and pet cats of course have common ancestors, but whereas the pedigree varieties have been developed by selective breeding, the pets are the result of free matings and conform to no special standards.

Their coats may be of any length and may be blotched, striped, patched or of one colour only. The eye colourings are frequently green or yellow and the noses long. Alert and usually very intelligent, they make charming pets. At many of the shows there are special classes for pets, and in most cases these are shown in beautiful condition. As there are no standards for them they are judged on their friendliness and condition.

Thousands of mongrels are working cats and are to be found on farms, docks, ships, in warehouses, and even working with pest control officials, for today as in the time of

Brown mackerel Tabby

Black and white pet cat

Tortoiseshell-and-white pet cat

the ancient Egyptians, the cat's worth as a catcher of mice and rats cannot be overlooked. Many of these cats are on the payroll, a weekly allowance being set aside for their food, as it is realized that no cat can live on vermin alone.

There are also, sad to say, thousands of strays, who live in derelict houses or roam the streets. Many are unwanted cats that have been turned out of their homes. While the various animal welfare societies play their part in trying to find new homes for them, there is all too often no alternative but to have them painlessly destroyed. This is why it must always be emphasized that neutering plays such an important part in keeping down the cat population.

NOTES ON CAT CARE

THE NEWLY ACQUIRED KITTEN

Having decided on the variety preferred, the next step is to find a kitten. This is not always easy, but pedigree kittens are sometimes advertised in the press. *Cats*, the official paper of the Governing Council of the Cat Fancy, gives club news, show dates and carries advertisements. The secretaries of cat clubs (*see* p. 183) may be able to help. A visit to a cat show is worth while, as all the varieties may be seen, some are offered for sale, and one can meet various breeders and perhaps book a kitten. The prices vary considerably and depend on whether the animal is for showing or breeding, or is simply a pet.

Non-pedigree kittens may be purchased for a small sum through local advertisements; from the animal welfare societies, or may be given away by friends and neighbours.

If one is unable to visit the breeder a kitten can be sent by train and picked up on arrival, but it is advisable to go and see the kittens at their home. A kitten should be 3–4 months when purchased, as at this age it should be fully weaned. The following points should be borne in mind: a wise choice is a kitten that is not nervous, is lively and alert, has bright eyes, clean ears, no signs of diarrhoea, feels sturdy to the touch, and has a well groomed flea-free coat.

On reaching home, the new owner should close all doors and windows, place guards in front of fires and cover chimney openings, and allow the kitten to explore the room quietly. He may feel lonely away from his mother and the rest of the litter. He must be introduced to things gradually by being carried around for a while and talked to, to gain his confidence, and when he has settled down may be offered a small tasty meal.

To pick up a kitten, place the hand under the body with the fingers up under the neck supporting the head. Never pick the kitten up by the scruff of the neck, and do not allow very young children to pull him about, or hug and squeeze him tightly, as this may cause injury.

Cats are naturally fastidious animals and a kitten of 3 months is probably already house-trained. For a sanitary tray an oven tin about 45cm (18 in) square is excellent. Sand, earth, peat moss, sawdust or one of the proprietary cat litters used to fill this, the tin should be placed on a layer of newspaper wide enough to protect the floor if the kitten scratches the contents out of the tray. The tray should be changed at least once daily and rinsed out with a suitable disinfectant – one that does not contain carbolic, which is poisonous to cats. The tray must be kept in the same place at least for a few days, so that the kitten can learn to find it. If a garden is available, the kitten can be taken out there at intervals and the sanitary tray moved nearer and nearer to the back door until the kitten is trained to go outside. This will take time and patience, but kittens learn quickly.

A cardboard box or basket with a warm blanket will make a good sleeping place, and if the weather is cold a warm hot-water-bottle will make the kitten feel less strange away from the warmth of the rest of the litter. A table-tennis ball, a toy mouse, a small soft toy or crumpled up piece of paper that can be chased around will help to keep him amused.

If a dog who is not used to cats is a member of the household when the new kitten arrives, great care and patience will be necessary for the first few days. Strangely enough the larger dog seems to be better behaved with a kitten, often washing and cleaning it. The smaller dog may be very jealous and resentful of the newcomer. Do not fondle the kitten in front of the dog or let him feel neglected. It is better not to feed them at the same time or to leave them alone together until friendly relations have been established. Unless the kitten has been brought up with dogs he will probably spit at the sight of the dog, who may start barking, frightening the kitten still more. Watch must be kept to see that if the kitten panics, his claws do not harm the dog's eyes. After a few days they will probably ignore each other, and then may even start to be friendly. In fact, cats and dogs can live in perfect harmony and be the best of friends.

FEEDING

A kitten of about 3 months requires four small meals a day. The more mixed the diet the better. An all-fish diet for example may cause a skin disease. Suitable foods include: raw beef given scraped or minced, cooked meat such as veal and lamb, cooked rabbit, chicken, a small quantity of liver, heart, cooked white fish, tinned cat food, tinned pilchards, raw egs mixed with one of the breakfast cereals such as corn flakes or a little crumbled brown bread.

The meals should be moist but not too wet, as excessive wetness tends to encourage diarrhoea. A heaped tablespoonful for each meal should be sufficient for the kitten, the quantity increasing as it grows. The early morning meal may be of porridge or of any of the well-known baby food preparations. Some kittens can take cows' milk without ill effects, but others may suffer with looseness after drinking it and in such a case it should be given very sparingly. There should always be fresh water to drink.

A few drops of halibut oil included in the daily diet will help to prevent rickets. Vegetables such as cabbage, carrots, spinach and green peas may be mashed up and given in small quantities with other foods. Care must be taken to see that all bones have been removed; on the other hand some kittens like to chew on a raw beef bone and this is perfectly safe.

The number of meals may be cut down gradually but increased in quantity until at about six months the kitten is having two large meals a day, according to appetite. Uneaten food should not be left down. A small milk drink could still be given at midday.

A cat or kitten that catches rats and mice still requires feeding, as a diet of vermin alone is not sufficient.

If a cat has no access to a garden or open fields, a pot of grass should be provided. This can be grown quite easily. Cats like to chew grass as a natural emetic which helps to prevent furballs. A weekly dose of a large teaspoonful of liquid paraffin is also helpful against this, particularly for the longhaired cats.

GROOMING

All cats need grooming, whether longhaired or shorthaired and whether pedigree or non-pedigree. The earlier it is started the better, as it will get the kitten used to being handled.

The general care is the same for all. The ears should be wiped out gently with slightly dampened cotton wool, and any dirt in the corner of the eyes also wiped away, using a fresh piece for each eye and ear. If the ears show any signs of ear mite (canker), or if there is a nasty smell from the ears, it is advisable to consult a vet. There are various forms of canker and to clear it up one has to use the appropriate treatment for the particular form one is dealing with.

As any cat may pick up an occasional flea, the fur should be combed through with a metal tooth-comb. A sure sign of fleas is the presence of very small black specks in the fur; these are the excreta of the fleas. Use an insecticide powder that is advertised as being suitable for cats. Stand the animals on a large sheet of newspaper, sprinkle the powder down into the roots of the fur and after about five minutes brush and comb all the powder out. Destroy the paper quickly or else tip all the fleas out of it into a jar filled with a solution of disinfectant. If you have found any fleas at all, repeat about a week later with the powder. The fur should be combed through daily.

Grooming a shorthaired cat is fairly simple. Hard hand grooming is all that is needed for most varieties, followed by a rub all over with a chamois leather, velvet or a piece of silk to produce a beautiful sheen. The fur should be combed through with a tooth-comb about once a week in case there are any fleas, but a wide-toothed comb should be avoided as it may make tracks in the fur, opening it up.

Grooming of the longhairs should be done daily, particularly in the spring and autumn, if the fur is not to mat up. Regular grooming removes the loose hairs which otherwise may be licked down when the cat is washing and may cause hairball. The coat should be combed through with a coarse steel comb, and any knots gently teased out with the fingers or a blunt-ended knitting needle. Talcum powder may be sprinkled into the fur and then brushed out. Powder is suitable only for the lighter coats. A little eau-de-cologne or a little bay rum can be used on the Blacks and other darker coats to remove the grease, followed with a polishing with velvet, chamois leather or silk. The frill around the head should be brushed up to form a frame for the face. The tail

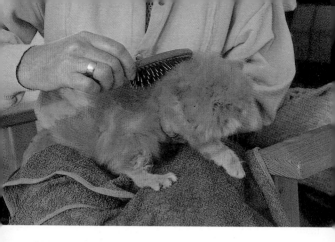

should receive special attention.

Cats that are to be exhibited may need extra grooming for a few weeks prior to a show, but care should be taken not to overgroom, so that the frill is pulled out and the coat is sparse. Prior to a show every trace of powder in the fur must be brushed out; if any is left in the coat on the day of the show it may lead to disqualification.

To get the fur into show condition, all dirt and grease must be removed. There must be no fleas or flea dirt, and the ears and eyes must be clean. In short, as well as being an outstanding specimen the cat must be in perfect health and groomed to the peak of perfection.

QUARANTINE AND IMPORT TO THE UNITED KINGDOM

On entering Britain from other countries all cats and kittens, without exception, must spend six months in a quarantine cattery approved by the Ministry of Agriculture, Fish and Food before going to live with their owners. Owners should remember that they will have to arrange this themselves in advance, completing the necessary forms to obtain permission to import the animal.

On arrival at the dock or airport of entry the animal must be met by an approved carrier and taken by the carrier (not by the owner) to the cattery. At the cattery an inoculation against rabies will be administered both on admission and prior to leaving. This is done whether the cat has been inoculated previously or not. The owner must bear the full cost.

Quarantine is thus an expensive proposition for the owner, and will not appeal to the cat either, as cats more than most animals seem to suffer from long solitary confinement. If a kitten is quarantined it will be fully grown before it is allowed home.

HOLIDAY ARRANGEMENTS

It should be borne in mind that arrangements will have to be made for the animal's welfare during holidays.

A neighbour may be willing to come into the home daily to feed the cat and shut it up at night. However, it is more advisable to let the cat stay in the house the whole time, and use a toilet tray, for cats miss their owners and if let out may

Boarding cattery

stray away looking for them. Alternatively friends may be willing to take the animal into their home, but again they should be warned that cats are escapists, and that doors and windows must be kept shut.

A boarding cattery may be the answer, but arrangements must be made well in advance as the catteries quickly get booked up, particularly the good ones. All boarding catteries in Britain have to be licensed, so make sure that the cattery of your choice does have a licence, and inspect where your cat will be kept before you make the booking.

The owner may be asked to show the cat's certificate of vaccination against feline infectious enteritis, and possibly to show a good health certificate from the vet.

It is advisable to supply a list of the cat's likes and dislikes to the cattery.

CAT AILMENTS

THE MORE SERIOUS ILLNESSES

Feline infectious enteritis   Caused by a virus, feline infectious enteritis (the clinical name is panleucopaenia) can be fatal, especially in kittens and young cats. Once very common both in pets and pedigree cats, it caused the death of hundreds of cats before safe and efficient vaccination techniques were developed, and these have now made epidemics rare. Control of secondary infections by use of antibiotics has helped to reduce the fatality rate.

The symptoms are a rise in temperature and rapid deterioration of condition, vomiting and lassitude. Veterinary treatment is urgently required if the animal's life is to be saved.

The veterinary surgeon will advise as to the correct age at which to give the vaccination. It is usually about ten weeks. Should the kitten die, all bedding should be burned, the house disinfected and no new kitten introduced for at least six months.

Cat flu   There are a number of respiratory diseases that are classed together and referred to as cat flu. They are very infectious and the viruses may be picked up at any time, sometimes at cat shows. It is not always fatal provided treatment is given in time, but careful nursing for many weeks will be necessary.

There are now several vaccinations against cat flu but because there are a number of different viruses, it is still not possible to guarantee protection against them all.

Symptoms include sneezing, discharge from the nose and eyes, ulcers in the mouth, coughing and a rise in temperature. The vet should be called in immediately to give treatment.

Feline infectious enteritis and cat flu are the most serious diseases that affect cats. There is also Feline Leukemia (Fel. V), a recently diagnosed illness. It can be contracted by prolonged contact with other infected cats and mainly affects multi-cat households. The symptoms are many and may include anaemia, tumours, breathing problems and diarrhoea.

A veterinary examination

Diagnosis is by examination of the blood, which can only be arranged by a veterinary surgeon. Cats do go down very rapidly when ill, and if a cat is not eating, is lethargic and loses interest in everything, veterinary advice should be sought as soon as possible. This can mean the difference between life and death in some cases.

Cat owners with a sick animal should never touch other cats or visit friends with young cats or kittens, or even write letters to them as infection can be carried by the paper.

MINOR AILMENTS

Abscesses   An abscess may be caused by an injury, blow, scratch or bite received in a cat fight. If the wound begins to heal with dirt inside, a swelling may develop. This is obviously painful and will prove to be full of pus.

Expert advice is needed to deal with an abscess, as an injection can possibly be given. Hot water fomentations or kaolin poultices may help to bring the swelling to a head, when it should be pricked with a sterilized needle. The wound should be kept open to ensure that all the pus is out. The fur will vanish around the wound but will quickly grow again.

An abscess on the ear is a different matter, as when the pus has drained from the flap of the ear it may crinkle up and spoil the appearance of the cat. Gentle massage daily with olive oil may help to prevent this.

Bad teeth   Dribbling in cats is often caused by a deposit of yellow tartar on the teeth, which also causes inflammation of the gums. Few people seem to appreciate the fact that cats do suffer with bad teeth, and a veterinary surgeon will remove these and also any yellow tartar.

Bites and stings   A bite or scratch received from another cat in a fight unfortunately very often turns into an abscess or a septic sore. Such bites or scratches should be bathed as soon as noticed with a mild disinfectant and watched carefully in case an abscess does develop.

Cats may be stung by bees or wasps, which they sometimes try to catch. In the case of a bee the sting will be left in the skin of the cat, and will have to be removed with a pair of tweezers. The place should be dabbed with a solution of bicarbonate of soda, or a blue washing bag. If the cat has been stung in the mouth it is advisable to contact a vet.

Bladder troubles   Males, neuters and infrequently females, with little opportunity for plenty of exercise, may be seen to strain and seem unable to pass water. Prompt medical advice is essential particularly if blood is passed. This may prove a serious condition and urgent treatment is required.

Canker   There are various kinds of canker, which is caused by ear mites in most cases, but the symptoms are practically the same. The cat will be seen scratching the ear and shaking its head, and an examination of the inside of the ear will reveal a brownish matter. It is advisable to consult the vet for the correct form of treatment.

Cold   A cat that is allowed to get below par in health readily catches cold and shows the ordinary symptoms of running eyes and sneezing. The cat should be isolated immediately in case these symptoms prove to be really the start of something more serious, kept warm and nursed carefully. The cold should be of short duration, and if it persists veterinary attention is advised.

Conjunctivitis   This is shown by an inflammation of the eyelids and a persistent discharge. A vet should be consulted straight away, as the condition may harm the eyes badly if allowed to continue. The newly opened eyes of a young kitten may have a little of the appearance of conjunctivitis, being sticky and inflamed. If they are gently wiped with dampened cotton wool and if a little Vaseline is applied to the eyelids this condition should soon clear up.

Constipation   A kitten may suffer from this after going to a new home, probably owing to the change of diet or to the fact that the kitten may be a little nervous and off food for a day or so. It is always best to get a diet sheet from the breeder and to stick to this until the kitten has settled down. New items may be introduced gradually. A teaspoonful of liquid paraffin or olive oil, which will probably be licked from the spoon without any trouble, should be given daily if the constipation is very bad. This with a varied diet should cure the condition, and there should be no further trouble. Older cats suffering from this should be given two teaspoonfuls and the food given a little moist rather than dry. Insufficient food may also cause this, and if this is suspected the amount of food should be increased gradually. A sardine or a little raw liver will often help.

Diarrhoea   Frequently when being weaned a kitten will have loose motions due to too much milk being given. A little kaolin powder given according to the chemist's instructions, together with cutting down the amount of liquid given, should help to correct this condition. Adult cats may also suffer in this way if they are unable to take milk. In these cases water only should be given to drink. If the condition persists professional advice should be sought.

Displaced eyelid   Cats have a third eyelid, the nictitating membrane, commonly referred to as the haw.

If the haws are plainly visible, it may signify that the animal is out of condition or is sickening for an illness. They usually go down again when the cat has regained its health, although occasionally after severe illness, they may remain slightly up permanently with no ill effects on the cat.

Eczema   There are various forms of this complaint, none contagious; some may be very irritating to the cat. Eczema can be an inherited tendency or else may prove to be caused by some item of the diet. Some cats are unable to drink milk or eat fish without showing some of the symptoms of eczema such as spots. In some cases it appears only in the spring and autumn. Milk of magnesia is generally useful. It also helps to reduce the amount of greasy or fatty foods and to make sure there is always plenty of clean water to drink. The veterinary surgeon will prescribe the correct treatment.

Fleas   The method of detecting and treating fleas is described on page 155 under *Grooming*. Any cat may occasionally pick up fleas, particularly in the countryside, where rabbits and hedgehogs run. If they persist in spite of treatment it may be that the cat is picking them up from their breeding ground, which is never on the host animal but on the ground somewhere. The sleeping box, blankets or wherever else the cat may sleep should be examined thoroughly and disinfected.

Fractures   It is rare for a cat to break a leg, but if it does happen as the result of an accident, an unlucky fall or a kick, the animal will show itself to be in pain and there will be a swelling; the limb will be held at an unusual angle. The animal should be restrained from moving as far as this is possible, and a veterinary surgeon called in to treat the broken limb.

Hairball   If a longhaired cat does not receive constant grooming to remove old fur from the coat, it may swallow a lot of the hair and a hairball may form in the stomach or bowels. Chewing grass, which is a natural emetic, may help the cat to bring up a lot of the hair. A weekly dose of liquid paraffin will also help to pass the hair through the cat. If the stomach looks distended and it is suspected that the animal has hairball, a veterinary surgeon should be consulted; if the condition does not respond to enemas an operation may be necessary.

Lameness   If a cat is seen to limp the pads should be closely examined to see if a thorn or prickle is causing the trouble. This should be gently removed with tweezers. A small wound or cut will require bathing with a mild antiseptic.

Long claws   A cat that has to live indoors a great deal should be provided with a rough log and trained to sharpen its claws on that to prevent them from growing too long. The claws of a cat living a normal life should need little attention, but if they do grow too long, the veterinary surgeon should be allowed to cut them. A cat should never be declawed.

Paint on coats   Not infrequently, and often through inquisitiveness, cats will get paint on their coats. This should not be treated with paraffin or turpentine, as they are poisonous to cats and will harm the animal's coat, causing the hair to fall out and the skin to become inflamed. It is better to cut off as much of the affected fur as possible, and allow the paint marks to grow out.

Poisons   Cats should be kept away from insecticide sprays used in the garden, and if weed killers are put down cats should not be allowed to walk on the places until they are washed well into the ground. The animals will lick their paws and coat and any insecticide, if not definitely poisonous, may cause stomach upsets.

Disinfectants containing creosote, which is very poisonous to cats, should not be used around the house. The use of rat poisons is not recommended if the cat may catch and eat the rats. Many rat poisons are accumulative, and the eating of several rats will cause trouble – if not death.

Ringworm   There are several forms of ringworm, which is not a worm but a fungus infection. It is highly contagious and can be freely transmitted from cats to people and the other way round. The infection can even be transferred from the queen to her kittens, after the queen herself has been given a completely successful cure. The kittens can develop the signs of the infection at a very early age. The fungus occurs in patches on the skin, and grows from the centre outwards in a ring pattern. It damages the hair roots and the hairs break off; the resulting ring of poor hair spoils the appearance of the coat. Patient treatment under medical supervision is required, and care must be taken to prevent any of the spores from spreading the infection further.

Tar on feet   When road repairs are in progress, the cat's feet may become covered with tar. The cat must not be allowed to lick it off, as it is a poison. The best emergency treatment is to wipe off as much as possible, and cover the pads with butter, gently rubbing until little tar remains.

Travel sickness   A few cats are badly affected when travelling in a car or train, dribbling all the time, and may even be sick. It is advisable not to feed them before a journey, and if it is known that the cat is liable to be upset the vet will probably prescribe some anti-sickness tablets.

Worms   Worms are found in most cats and if allowed to persist may result in a deterioration in the cat's health. There are two kinds of worms: tape worms, which may come away in segments and resemble grains of rice, and the round worms which look like pieces of thin string. It is not necessary to starve the cat before worming nowadays. There are many remedies on the market, but it is really best for the vet to prescribe, as the amount to be given depends on the age and weight of the cat or kitten, and much harm may be done through indiscriminate treatment.

CAT BREEDING

CALLING AND MATING

A female cat may come into season or 'on heat' and start calling at anything from six months onwards. Siamese and other foreign varieties may call earlier than the longhairs, as may non-pedigree pets. This does not mean that the female (known as the queen) is old enough to be mated. Most breeders agree that the queen should be at least ten months old; and that queens should not be mated until they have called at least once before.

It should be the aim of every breeder to produce the best kittens possible, and so the chosen stud should be of good type, with a good pedigree. Wherever possible his good points should correspond to any bad points in the queen, and so give the chance of eliminating them in the offspring. Not every breeder can produce a champion every time, but many do produce very good kittens through careful breeding.

The first signs shown by the female that she is about to start calling may be restlessness and extra friendliness. She may start rushing around, mewing, and treading the ground with her back legs, sometimes rolling over and over and howling. She must be kept away from all male cats if she is to be sent to stud. Females come into season frequently, usually in the spring and summer, but some may call all the year round. With most there is about four weeks between the calls, which may last anything from three to ten days. A queen should be allowed to have no more than two litters in the season; many breeders prefer to set the limit at one litter – although with the Siamese this can be difficult. The queen should not be mated immediately after bringing up a litter, but must be allowed to get back into first-class condition.

The queen should be taken to the chosen stud on the second day of her call, but only after the stud owner has been contacted to ensure that it is convenient. She will probably be given two matings by the stud, in case the first was not adequate. If no kittens ensue the male's owner may be willing to take the queen again, but there is no obligation to do so.

Mating

The queen's owner will be given a copy of the male's pedigree, the date of the mating and probable date of kittening.

On her return it is important to keep her away from all male cats for a week or more if still calling, to prevent any further mating, for this could cause a double conception to take place, and the resulting litter would be sired by two males.

KITTENING

The queen should be treated just as normal during the pregnancy, given a varied and nourishing diet, and given a little milk of magnesia in any milk or milky foods to correct any possible acidity. The kittens may be expected in about 65 days, but this is only approximate.

After about three weeks a slight reddening of the nipples is usually seen, and during the last four weeks the cat will increase in girth, and will be most unmistakably in kitten. Small doses of olive or vegetable oil are most helpful during pregnancy, about a teaspoonful once or twice a week.

A week or two before the kittens are due, provide a large box, but not so large that the kittens can roll away into a

Kittens' mealtime

corner and get cold, nor so high that the queen has trouble jumping in and out, for she may jump on the kittens when getting back. The box should be in a darkish corner or cupboard away from any possible interference, especially from young children. It is wise to put plenty of newspaper in the box, which the queen will probably shred into pieces, almost making a nest. She may need watching during the last day or two, as she may decide she would rather have the kittens in her owner's bed or some other impossible place.

When the kittens are about to be born, there may be signs of milk in the nipple and the cat may be extra affectionate. She should settle down happily in the box, probably purring all the time, and apart from an occasional glance, it is better to leave her alone, and she will probably be able to cope with everything by herself. If after some hours no kittens arrive and she is still straining, veterinary advice should be sought. When it appears all the kittens have arrived, the queen having washed and cleaned up everything should be given a warm milk drink and fresh bedding, and left in peace. If the queen is a good mother, the kittens should need no attention for the next ten or twelve days, apart from the occasional look to see if they are all doing well. She should be on a light diet for about 24 hours after kittening.

The same diet and facilities of course will be appropriate for the birth of any kittens, whether planned by the breeder or otherwise, and whether pedigree or non-pedigree.

Once born, and as long as their mother does not object to their being handled, the kittens may be sexed (*see below*). Any unwanted kittens should be taken to the veterinary surgeon or to one of the animal welfare societies where they will be destroyed humanely, instead of being drowned, as this is very cruel.

The mother should be allowed to keep at least one kitten; it may be decided that further kittens are not wanted, and if so once the kitten has been fully weaned arrangements can be made to have the mother spayed (*see* p. 173).

THE KITTENS

Many owners have a shock on seeing their first pedigree litters, as they sometimes look just like mongrels. Blue Persians and many other self-coloured longhaired kittens start off with clear tabby markings, which fade as the long fur grows. Blacks may begin with a brownish colour and Chinchilla kittens are dark; Siamese kittens are white.

Sexing should be done when the kittens are a day or two old, as the fur will not have grown too much. Beneath the tail of the male kitten will be seen the anus, and about three-eighths to half an inch nearer the stomach the rudimentary testicles, which have a bunchy appearance, may be seen. In the female the anus is in the same position, but close to it the vagina appears as a small slit. There is no 'bunchiness' in the female. If both sexes are in the litter the task is easier, as the differences may be seen more clearly with male and female side by side.

Most queens can manage to feed up to four or five kittens quite successfully. Some manage more. If it is found that a queen has no milk, it may be possible to find a foster mother, otherwise hand-feeding may be necessary. This is no easy task, as it means feeding every two hours day and night for nearly three weeks. If the queen has lost interest in the kittens, they must be cleaned very gently all over by wiping with a slightened dampened rough towelling to replace the mother's tongue.

About eight to twelve days after birth depending on the breed, the kittens' eyes will start to open. If there appears any stickiness on their eyelids and the eyes are still shut after this time, they should be gently wiped with a little cotton wool, and the lids smeared with a little Vaseline. If this fails, the vet can supply special ointment which should clear up any trouble. The kittens should not be kept in any strong light until the eyes are well opened.

At the age of about three weeks the kittens will start to climb out of the box and stagger around. A small easily accessible toilet tray should be provided, and they will soon start using it.

Weaning may start at this age. Suitable foods are milk food sold specially for kittens, baby foods or goats' milk; a little milk of magnesia may be added to prevent digestive trouble. A drop of the food on the kitten's lips for the first day or two will enable it to get the taste. Most kittens readily learn to lap from a spoon, which in turn can lead to a small saucer. A small teaspoonful should be sufficient once a day for the first week; in the second week a second feed can be introduced, offering perhaps a little scraped raw beef.

Baby foods cereals may be introduced gradually, and first solids may include cooked white fish, scraped raw beef, mashed cooked rabbit, cornflakes, raw or scrambled eggs. A kitten's stomach is very small and there is a risk of overfeeding as the kitten will also be suckling from its mother. By the age of eight weeks, weaning should be completed and the kitten should receive four or five small meals a day.

Pedigree kittens may be sold from about 12 weeks old, non-pedigree kittens from perhaps eight weeks. At this point a little needs to be said about the paperwork that is involved in cat breeding.

If one wishes to sell pedigree kittens, one will need to have the pedigrees ready to show to the buyers, and to hand over as part of the sale. These are to be obtained from the specialist cat clubs.

If one intends to become a cat breeder it will be worth while to register a prefix with the Governing Council of the Cat Fancy. The prefix is a distinguishing name which a breeder uses in giving a kitten a name. To register a prefix one has to be a member of a cat club. Prefixes have to be approved and granted by the Governing Council of the Cat Fancy and once registered may not be used by any other breeder. The prefix is inserted on the pedigree and on the registration form.

Apart from the prefix, the kittens themselves will need to be registered with the Governing Council, as will their transfer to a new owner if they are sold. A fee is payable for all registrations, including the registration of transfers.

Advertisements of kittens for sale may be placed in *Cats* or in the local newspapers. A breeder's name will become known through exhibiting in shows, particularly if at all successfully, and this may bring in orders for kittens.

THE STUD

Naturally, in the breeding of pedigree cats the stud is of paramount importance. It might be thought that all that is necessary is to buy a pair of unrelated kittens, one of which is male and the other female. This may be all right in theory but the practical difficulties are many. For example, the pair might well live happily together for a few months, but when the female starts to call the male might not be nearly mature enough to mate her; and conversely, the male may mature well ahead of the female. Apart from this there are many cases where males and females who have grown up together never do mate together, although the male may well mate other females.

For these reasons it is common for a breeder to take the females to a stud elsewhere.

A male should not be used for stud until about a year old, and some are not ready until over two years. A virile stud will not be content with just one female to mate, and if allowed complete freedom may well roam the district, looking for more females. This might lead to his catching some infection, or else he might get involved in fights, in which he could even be seriously injured.

Any male not needed for breeding should be neutered when old enough. This may be from 4½ months upwards, but the vet will advise on this. If not neutered, before long he will

A stud home and run

start to spray, leaving the strong tom-cat smell everywhere.

To keep a stud it will be necessary to provide a large sized stud house and a very big run. It should not be too near the house or neighbours' houses, because of the smell and the possible cat noises that will be heard. On the other hand, he should be within easy sight of the owner, so that he may see comings and goings, and can be talked to, and should also be allowed to roam the garden under supervision. In the winter when there are no calling queens around some males do live in the house without spraying, but they have to be watched. Studs are usually very friendly and sociable, and certainly should not be kept in complete isolation.

In choosing a male kitten to raise as a stud one should ensure that he is as near the required standard for his variety as possible, and that he has a good pedigree. The more winning the kitten has done, the higher the price.

If the breeder has three or four queens these may be sufficient to keep the male happy; otherwise it would be kinder to accept one or two queens from other breeders for stud. For the owner this entails spending many hours in the stud's house to ensure matings have taken place, and there is always the risk of infection from the visitors. Naturally, the male should be inoculated against feline infectious enteritis, and no queens should be accepted without a veterinary certificate showing that they have had this very necessary inoculation. A visiting queen should always be thoroughly examined before being put in the stud's house to ensure that she is in first class condition, and has no fleas or any signs of skin troubles in the fur.

Before queens can be accepted, part of the stud's house must be made into a separate sleeping compartment with small run for the females. The run should be covered with wire netting to enable the pair to see one another without actually meeting, and the sleeping part should have a solid door, to ensure the female some privacy. A shelf should be provided to enable the male to jump out of the female's way once she has mated, as some may be vicious and attack the male immediately afterwards. Two matings are usually given in case the first has not taken.

NEUTERING AND SPAYING

If they are not intended for breeding, cats are prevented from doing so by means of the operations of neutering, castrating males and spaying females. The right age at which to have the operation depends on the rate of the kitten's development, and may be from three and a half months upwards for males and four and a half months upwards for females. The veterinary surgeon's advice should be taken about this.

As an anaesthetic is used in both cases, no food or drink should be given for at least twelve hours before the operation. A male kitten usually recovers very quickly, but should be given light food for the next day or so and kept quiet. A female's spaying is a little more serious, requiring a small incision and a few stitches, but with good surgery and after-care nursing, the female soon recovers and does not suffer any ill effect.

Many owners are hesitant about having their cats neutered, thinking they may get too fat and lethargic, but there is no reason why they should if they are fed correctly and have plenty of attention, ample exercise and plenty of playthings. The majority of neuters are just as lively and intelligent as any 'entire' animal; and the advantage is that there is no unpleasant smell from the males, nor do the females call incessantly or keep trying to get out of the house to find a suitable mate.

BREEDING TABLE

This table is only a rough guide as individual cats vary in length of gestation. Also, allowances have to be made in leap years. In each pair of columns, date on left when mated, date on right when kittens due.

Mated	Due	Mated	Due	Mated	Due	Mated	Due	Mated	Due	Mated	Due
Jan.	Mar.	Feb.	Apr.	Mar.	May	Apr.	June	May	July	June	Aug.
1	7	1	7	3	7	2	6	2	6	1	5
2	8	2	8	4	8	3	7	3	7	2	6
3	9	3	9	5	9	4	8	4	8	3	7
4	10	4	10	6	10	5	9	5	9	4	8
5	11	5	11	7	11	6	10	6	10	5	9
6	12	6	12	8	12	7	11	7	11	6	10
7	13	7	13	9	13	8	12	8	12	7	11
8	14	8	14	10	14	9	13	9	13	8	12
9	15	9	15	11	15	10	14	10	14	9	13
10	16	10	16	12	16	11	15	11	15	10	14
11	17	11	17	13	17	12	16	12	16	11	15
12	18	12	18	14	18	13	17	13	17	12	16
13	19	13	19	15	19	14	18	14	18	13	17
14	20	14	20	16	20	15	19	15	19	14	18
15	21	15	21	17	21	16	20	16	20	15	19
16	22	16	22	18	22	17	21	17	21	16	20
17	23	17	23	19	23	18	22	18	22	17	21
18	24	18	24	20	24	19	23	19	23	18	22
19	25	19	25	21	25	20	24	20	24	19	23
20	26	20	26	22	26	21	25	21	25	20	24
21	27	21	27	23	27	22	26	22	26	21	25
22	28	22	28	24	28	23	27	23	27	22	26
23	29	23	29	25	29	24	28	24	28	23	27
24	30	24	30	26	30	25	29	25	29	24	28
25	31			27	31	26	30	26	30	25	29
								27	31	26	30
		May								27	31
Apr.		25	1	**June**		**July**					
26	1	26	2	28	1	27	1	**Aug.**			
27	2	27	3	29	2	28	2			**Sept.**	
28	3	28	4	30	3	29	3	28	1	28	1
29	4	**Mar.**		31	4	30	4	29	2	29	2
30	5	1	5	**Apr.**		**May**		30	3	30	3
31	6	2	6	1	5	1	5	31	4		

Mated (July)	Due (Sept.)	Mated (Aug.)	Due (Oct.)	Mated (Sept.)	Due (Nov.)	Mated (Oct.)	Due (Dec.)	Mated (Nov.)	Due (Jan.)	Mated (Dec.)	Due (Feb.)
1	4	1	5	1	5	1	5	1	5	1	4
2	5	2	6	·2	6	2	6	2	6	2	5
3	6	3	7	3	7	3	7	3	7	3	6
4	7	4	8	4	8	4	8	4	8	4	7
5	8	5	9	5	9	5	9	5	9	5	8
6	9	6	10	6	10	6	10	6	10	6	9
7	10	7	11	7	11	7	11	7	11	7	10
8	11	8	12	8	12	8	12	8	12	8	11
9	12	9	13	9	13	9	13	9	13	9	12
10	13	10	14	10	14	10	14	10	14	10	13
11	14	11	15	11	15	11	15	11	15	11	14
12	15	12	16	12	16	12	16	12	16	12	15
13	16	13	17	13	17	13	17	13	17	13	16
14	17	14	18	14	18	14	18	14	18	14	17
15	18	15	19	15	19	15	19	15	19	15	18
16	19	16	20	16	20	16	20	16	20	16	19
17	20	17	21	17	21	17	21	17	21	17	20
18	21	18	22	18	22	18	22	18	22	18	21
19	22	19	23	19	23	19	23	19	23	19	22
20	23	20	24	20	24	20	24	20	24	20	23
21	24	21	25	21	25	21	25	21	25	21	24
22	25	22	26	22	26	22	26	22	26	22	25
23	26	23	27	23	27	23	27	23	27	23	26
24	27	24	28	24	28	24	28	24	28	24	27
25	28	25	29	25	29	25	29	25	29	25	28
26	29	26	30	26	30	26	30	26	30		**Mar.**
27	30	27	31		**Dec.**	27	31	27	31	26	1
			Nov.	27	1		**Jan.**		**Feb.**	27	2
28		28	1	28	2	28	1	28	1	28	3
29		29	2	29	3	29	2	29	2	29	4
30		30	3	30	4	30	3	30	3	30	5
31		31	4			31	4			31	6

CAT SHOWS AND SHOWING

There are many cat shows all over Britain, where a great number of pedigree cats and kittens, and even some pet cats, compete for a great variety of cups, championships, prize cards or rosettes. Show dates are published in *Cats*, which is obtained through a newsagent. Otherwise a list of the shows may be obtained from the Secretary of the Governing Council (*see* p. 181).

The shows are organized by various cat clubs under the auspices of the Governing Council. They are in three categories: championship, sanction and exemption shows. An exemption show is a primary event which a club will put on before running a sanction. The rules are not so stringent as in the higher shows and a novice might well exhibit first in one of these in order to learn what showing is all about. Frequently well-known judges officiate and after judging they are usually willing to give owners a personal opinion of the cats and kittens.

Sanction shows in turn are effectively rehearsals for the championship shows, and are run very much on the same lines as the championship shows except that challenge certificates are not given.

The major events are the championship shows, where challenge certificates are to be won. Only the open class winner in each variety is eligible for a challenge certificate and even then the award is made only if the judges are satisfied that the required standard has been met.

Championship shows vary in size from the smaller shows, which may have about 300 entries, to the National Cat Club show, held in London every year, where over 2,000 cats are exhibited. Another big show is the Kensington Kitten and Neuter Cat Club show, at the end of July. As this is for kittens and neuters only, no challenge certificates can be awarded. For outstanding neuters, premier certificates are given. The Governing Council of the Cat Fancy holds an important event known as the Supreme Show, at which exhibits may be eligible only if they have previously won at a show.

To become a champion a cat must come first in an open

A National Cat Club Show

class of its own variety and be awarded a challenge certificate
for each win at three shows under three different judges. A
champion may become a grand champion by winning the
Champion of Champions class on three occasions under
similar conditions.

To become a premier a neuter must be first in the open
neuter classes and be awarded a premier certificate for each
win at three shows under different judges. It may become a
grand premier by winning the Premier of Premiers class on
three occasions under similar conditions.

ASSESSMENT CLASSES

For many years cats and kittens whose colouring, coat or
type did not conform to any recognized standard were
registered as follows: if longhairs, 13a: Any Other Colour; if
shorthairs, 26: Any Other Variety; if new colours of Siamese,
32x. However, this has given rise to large classes of cats at
the shows for which no standards were available. Since these
cats are in effect selectively bred new varieties they are now
placed on an experimental register. Preliminary standards
are drafted for any such varieties, with tentative numbers.

These standards are displayed with the animals at the shows, in what are known as the Assessment classes. The entries are judged on their individual merits and not in competition with each other. They are also allowed to enter in appropriate miscellaneous classes. If a cat is considered good enough it is awarded a merit card, and the number of merit cards awarded counts towards the eventual recognition of the variety.

If sufficient numbers of a new variety are bred, and to a high enough standard, the breed may be given provisional recognition and a breed number and its own classes at a show. For a provisionally recognized breed no championship is awarded. Full recognition and championship status may be granted only when at least 100 specimens of a variety have been bred to the required standard.

ENTERING A CAT FOR SHOW

It is not necessary to belong to a cat club to show a cat, but most clubs put on special prizes for their members only, at their own show and at other shows. At least a couple of months before a show, any entrant who is not a member of a club should apply to the show manager for a schedule, which gives details of the various classes and prizes. The entry, with the correct money, should be returned well before the closing date, which is about six weeks before the show. It is advisable to send in the entry early, as most shows can only accept a certain number of cats and kittens, and may have to return a number of entries even if received before the closing date.

A number of shows put on classes for non-pedigree household pets, which need not be registered, but any pedigree exhibit, whether cat, kitten or neuter, must be registered with the Governing Council and must have belonged to the person exhibiting for at least three weeks prior to the show.

Some shows send out numbered tallies and vetting-in cards a week or two before the show, others may give them out on the day. Cats must be taken to the show in escape-proof baskets or boxes, and must never be carried in the arms. They must be accompanied to the show and may not be sent by rail direct to the show, as used to happen some time ago. All entries have to be examined by a veterinary surgeon before they may be penned in the show hall, and if there are fleas in the coat, dirty ears, any symptoms of the start of an illness, or a skin complaint, the cat will not be allowed to be shown and the entry fees will be forfeit.

After passing through the vetting-in the exhibit may be taken into the hall and placed in the pen bearing the same number as the tally. Before doing this it is advisable to wipe the bars of the pen with a mild non-toxic disinfectant or a little methylated spirit. A plain white unmarked blanket, together with a white toilet tray are the only things allowed in the pen. Litter should be brought for this, or newspaper, as some exhibitors prefer.

Before giving a final grooming (but do not use powder in the hall) check that the tally is safely around the cat's neck on plain white tape or ribbon. Exhibitors must not approach the pen while the cat is being judged.

There are usually a great variety of classes, including the open, breeders, novices, junior and senior, as well as any that the clubs may put on specially for their own members only. As the classes are judged the award slips are put on a board to enable the exhibitors to know the results. After lunch the award cards are put on the pens; then the cats may be fed and the exhibitors may collect any prize money they have won. Most shows close at about 5.30 p.m.

On reaching home one should wipe the cat's coat over with a mild non-toxic disinfectant, using a much diluted solution for the eyes, mouth, ears and paws. Some people give their exhibits half a teaspoon of whisky or brandy in a little milk. Even if the cat has been inoculated against feline infectious enteritis (and no cat may be shown without this inoculation) there are still some other infections that might be picked up, and a disinfecting may give protection against these.

After this the cat should be given a meal and then, having been penned all day, it will probably rush madly around for a while. It should however be isolated for the next few days as a precaution against passing on any infection it may chance to have picked up.

Pet cats may be exhibited at certain shows which put on

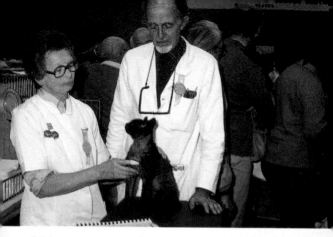

special classes for them. They are judged mainly on their condition and friendliness, as there are no recognized standards. Many beautiful cats are seen at the shows, really doing credit to their owners. There are also classes for cats with one pedigree parent and one unknown.

JUDGING AND STEWARDING

There is no easy road to becoming a judge. It means years of stewarding and usually also of breeding a particular variety, thus becoming competent to judge it. Judges for Siamese and the longhairs are appointed by joint advisory committees made up of the most experienced judges already in service. For the other shorthaired varieties the breed clubs appoint judges, usually to start as probationers. This is the system in countries like Britain where cat breeding is a well established tradition, whereas in some other countries where cat breeding is new, judges are selected by a system of examinations.

A steward's duties begin with arriving in good time on the morning of the show armed with pen, pencil and rubber, finding the judge's table and making sure that the disinfectant spray bottle provided is filled and that paper towels are available for cleaning the judge's hands in between handling the exhibits. The steward should check that for each cat the tally around its neck and the pen number are the same. Handling the exhibits with care, the steward must place them on the table ready for the judge to see and assess. A further duty is to check that the awards that are given correspond exactly with what the judge has written on the slips in the book. The slips must be signed by the judge before being taken up to the Show Secretary's table.

A good steward's capabilities will soon come to be noticed and eventually the name put forward as a possible judge.

THE GOVERNING COUNCIL OF THE CAT FANCY

The Council is a democratically formed body composed of delegates from all the cat clubs and societies that are affiliated to it (*see* p. 183). The delegates are elected annually by the members of the clubs. The objects of the Council are to provide for the registration of cats and pedigrees, to classify cat breeds and varieties, to approve the dates of cat shows, to improve cat breeding and to protect the welfare of cats and the interests of cat owners generally; but not to be involved in any financial transactions connected with cats.

As well as keeping the register of cats and issuing the certificates for pedigree cats, the Council registers transfers from one owner to another. It is responsible for the granting of challenge certificates to winning cats at championship shows. It approves the standards and allocations of points for all breeds.

The Council publishes a stud book from time to time, in which breeding details and the achievements at shows of all prize-winning cats are given.

The Council deals with all general matters concerning the Cat Fancy, and issues a list of shows held each year under its jurisdiction. It publishes a full Official Standard of Points which includes all the recognised breeds of cats approved by it and the points allocated to the individual characteristics. Also included are the various breeds, long and short coated, which have preliminary and provisional recognition, and which should eventually reach Championship status. Enquire about the price of each from:

The Governing Council of the Cat Fancy
4–6 Penel Orlieu, Bridgwater, Somerset TA6 3PG.

CAT CLUBS AND SOCIETIES

All Breed Clubs
Bedford and District Cat Club
Bucks, Oxon and Berks Cat
   Society
Cheshire Area Cat Club
Chester and North Wales Cat
   Club
Coventry and Leicester Cat
   Club
Croydon Cat Club
Cumberland Cat Club
Cumbria Cat Club
Durham County Cat Club
Edinburgh and East of Scotland
   Cat Club
Essex Cat Club
Gwynedd Cat Club
Heart of England Cat Club
Herts and Middx Cat Club
Humberside Cat Club
Jersey Cat Club
Kensington Kitten and Neuter
   Cat Club
Kentish Cat Society
Kernow Cat Club
Lancashire Cat Club
Lincolnshire Cat Club
Maidstone Area Cat Club
Merseyside Cat Club
Midland Counties Cat Club
National Cat Club
Nor' East of Scotland Cat Club
Northern Counties Cat Club
Northern Ireland Cat Club
North West Cat Club
Notts and Derbys Cat Club
Oxford and District Cat Club
Preston and Blackpool Cat Club
Scottish Cat Club
Second City Cat Club
Shropshire Cat Club
Southern Counties Cat Club

South London Cat Club
Suffolk and Norfolk Cat Club
Surrey and Sussex Cat
   Association
Teesside Cat Club
Three Counties Cat Club
Ulster Siamese and All Breed
   Cat Club
Wessex Cat Club
West of England and South
   Wales Cat Club
Yorkshire Cat Club

Specific Breed Clubs
Abyssinian Cat Association
Abyssinian Cat Club
Angora Cat Club
Balinese Society
Birman Cat Club
Black and White Cat Club
Black, Red Self and
   Tortoiseshell Cat Club
Blue Persian Cat Society
Blue-Point Siamese Cat Club
British and Manx Shorthair Cat
   Association
British Shorthair Tipped Club
Burmese Breeders Society
Burmese Cat Club
Cameo, Pewter and Smoke
   Society
Capital Longhair Cat
   Association
Celtic Longhair Cat Association
Chinchilla, Silver Tabby and
   Smoke Cat Association
Chocolate and Lilac Persian Cat
   Society
Chocolate Point Siamese Cat
   Club
Colourpoint Cat Club

Colourpoint Rex Coated AOV Cat Club

Colourpoint Society of Great Britain

East Anglian Persian Cat Society

Foreign White Cat Fanciers Association

Foreign White Cat Society

Havana and Foreign Lilac Cat Club

Havana, Foreign and Oriental Cat Association

Korat Group

Lilac-Pointed Siamese Cat Society

Longhair Cream and Blue Cream Cat Association

Longhaired Cat Club

Midshires Siamese Cat Association

North of Britain Longhaired Cat Club

Northern Siamese Cat Society

Oriental Tabby Cat Club

Red, Cream, Tortoiseshell, Tortoiseshell-and-white, Blue Cream and Brown Tabby Society

Rex Cat Club

Russian Blue Breeders Association

Seal-Point Siamese Cat Club

Shorthaired Cat Society

Siamese Cat Association

Siamese Cat Club

Siamese Cat Society of Scotland

Siamese Cat Society of the British Empire

Tabby Cat Club

Tabby Point Siamese and Progressive Breeders Cat Club

Tabby Pointed Siamese Cat Society

Tortoiseshell and White and Bicolour Cat Club

Ulster Siamese and All Breed Cat Club

United Chinchilla Association

6 & 6^A Smoke Society

729 Society

For a full list of clubs with secretaries' names and addresses, apply to the G.C.C.F. at the address given on page 182.

THE ANATOMY OF A CAT

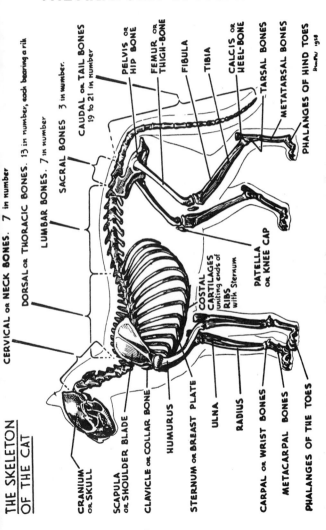

THE SKELETON OF THE CAT

CERVICAL or NECK BONES. 7 in number

DORSAL or THORACIC BONES. 13 in number, each bearing a rib

LUMBAR BONES. 7 in number

SACRAL BONES. 3 in number.

CAUDAL or TAIL BONES 19 to 21 in number

PELVIS or HIP BONE

FEMUR or THIGH-BONE

FIBULA

TIBIA

CALCIS or HEEL-BONE

TARSAL BONES

METATARSAL BONES

PHALANGES OF HIND TOES

PATELLA or KNEE CAP

CRANIUM or SKULL

SCAPULA or SHOULDER BLADE

CLAVICLE or COLLAR BONE

HUMURUS

STERNUM or BREAST PLATE

COSTAL CARTILAGES uniting ends of RIBS with Sternum

ULNA

RADIUS

CARPAL or WRIST BONES

METACARPAL BONES

PHALANGES OF THE TOES

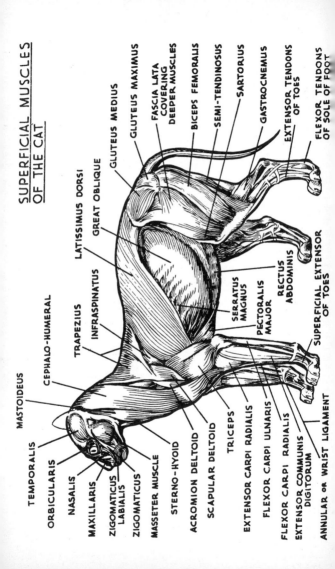

SUPERFICIAL MUSCLES OF THE CAT

TEMPORALIS
ORBICULARIS
NASALIS
MAXILLARIS
ZIGOMATICUS LABIALIS
ZIGOMATICUS
MASSETER MUSCLE
STERNO-HYOID
ACROMION DELTOID
SCAPULAR DELTOID
TRICEPS
EXTENSOR CARPI RADIALIS
FLEXOR CARPI ULNARIS
FLEXOR CARPI RADIALIS
EXTENSOR COMMUNIS DIGITORUM
ANNULAR or WRIST LIGAMENT

MASTOIDEUS
CEPHALO-HUMERAL
TRAPEZIUS
INFRASPINATUS
LATISSIMUS DORSI
GREAT OBLIQUE

SERRATUS MAGNUS
PECTORALIS MAJOR
SUPERFICIAL EXTENSOR OF TOES
RECTUS ABDOMINIS

GLUTEUS MEDIUS
GLUTEUS MAXIMUS
FASCIA LATA COVERING DEEPER MUSCLES
BICEPS FEMORALIS
SEMI-TENDINOSUS
SARTORIUS
GASTROCNEMUS
EXTENSOR TENDONS OF TOES
FLEXOR TENDONS OF SOLE OF FOOT

INDEX

Numbers in **bold** refer to illustrations